וְאָהַבְתָּ לְרֵעֲךָ כָּמוֹךָ

Love Your Neighbor, Love Yourself

Building Healthy Relationships

A Joint Project with Jewish Women International

Karen L. Stein, Editor
Amy Dorsch, Assistant Editor

UNITED SYNAGOGUE YOUTH – UNITED SYNAGOGUE OF CONSERVATIVE JUDAISM

UNITED SYNAGOGUE OF CONSERVATIVE JUDAISM

UNITED SYNAGOGUE YOUTH

Jules A. Gutin	DIRECTOR
Karen L. Stein	ASSISTANT DIRECTOR
Aviva Tilles	PROJECTS DIRECTOR
Ilan Schwartz	PROGRAM COORDINATOR
Adam Kofinas	MEETINGS MANAGER
Amy Greenfeld	EDUCATION COORDINATOR
Matthew Halpern	COMMUNICATIONS COORDINATOR
Nahum Binder	CENTRAL SHALIACH
David Keren	DIRECTOR, ISRAEL PROGRAMS
Yitzchak Jacobsen	DIRECTOR, ISRAEL OFFICE
Yossi Garr	DIRECTOR, NATIV

INTERNATIONAL YOUTH COMMISSION

Paul Kochberg, CHAIRPERSON
Jonathan S. Greenberg, Vice CHAIRPERSON

UNITED SYNAGOGUE OF CONSERVATIVE JUDAISM

Richard Skolnik, INTERNATIONAL PRESIDENT
Rabbi Steven Wernick, EXECUTIVE VICE PRESIDENT
Richard S. Moline, DIRECTOR, DEPARTMENT OF YOUTH AND YOUNG ADULT SERVICES
Dr. Marilyn Lishnoff Wind, VICE PRESIDENT FOR YOUTH SERVICES AND EDUCATION

A publication of the International Youth Commission
United Synagogue of Conservative Judaism
820 Second Avenue, New York, NY 10017
http://www.uscj.org/usy

First Edition, 2009

Printed and bound in the United States of America by Howard Press
Cover design by Matthew Halpern
Production, layout and design by Karen L. Stein, Project Editor

Table Of Contents

Editor's Note

Message from JWI

Part One: Love Your Neighbor, Love Yourself.. 1

    Chapter One: Community... 5

    Chapter Two: Friendship... 17

Part Two: Bein Adam L'Atzmo—A Look at Oneself.............................. 37

    Chapter Three: Individuality and Equality.............................. 39

    Chapter Four: RESPECT—Find Out What It Means To Me........ 51

    Chapter Five: Our Bodies, Our Souls...................................... 61

    Chapter Six: Being a Mensch.. 75

    Chapter Seven: The Power of Words...................................... 81

Part Three: Bein Adam L'Chavero—Between Friends........................ 101

    Chapter Eight: Dating... 103

    Chapter Nine: Marriage.. 115

    Chapter Ten: Physical Intimacy.. 119

Part Four: Beauty and Its Beast—Conflict in Relationships............ 141

    Chapter Eleven: Harmony and Conflict................................. 143

    Chapter Twelve: When Love Hurts... 161

    Chapter Thirteen: Decision Making and Peer Pressure......... 171

Conclusion.. 181

Bibliography... 183

From The Editor's Pen

V'ahavta L'rayecha Kamocha —Love Your Neighbor, Love Yourself.
How do you strengthen your relationships with others? How do you look at your use of language, your self as holy and your role within the community? What can you do to help ensure that others will have healthy relationships? What happens when a relationship takes a turn for the worse? As we turn the pages of this book, we will explore these questions and we will ask many more.

We are pleased that we have been able to partner with Jewish Women International on this sourcebook and are excited to be able to bring these important questions and issues to the table. Lori Weinstein, executive director, and her team at JWI, has taken a strong leadership role in educating about relational aggressions and how teenagers can better equip themselves to be in healthy relationships. The expertise of Deborah Rosenbloom, director of programs at JWI, as author and educator was evident throughout this sourcebook, particularly in the fourth part of the book on conflict and relationships. When I first sat with Deborah, to develop the contents of this book, we had a blank page in front of us. We started simply with the question: "What is a healthy relationship?" It was not long before we realized that we could not deal with healthy relationships with others until we also considered how we relate to ourselves.

This book is divided into four sections: Part One: Love Your Neighbor, Love Yourself addresses issues of community and friendship. Part Two: Bein Adam L'Atzmo– Between a Person and Oneself explores intrapersonal issues of individualism, equality, *menschlikite*, and the power of language. In Part Three: Bein Adam L'Chavero— Between Friends, we will explore our interpersonal relationships including dating, marriage and physical intimacy. In the final section, we explore some of the issues of unhealthy relationships including bullying and relational aggression, and conclude with a chapter on decision making.

The final product of "Love Your Neighbor, Love Yourself" wove together materials written and compiled by Deborah Rosenbloom and Rella Kaplowitz (formerly of JWI) as well as a wealth of material previously published by USY, including sources on relationships and body image from "In God's Image: Making Jewish Decisions About the Body," by Dr. Bernard Novick, z"l; sources on friendship and l'shon hara from USY's publication, "Derech Eretz," by Rabbi Ron Isaacs; and on dating and marriage from USY's publication, "The Jewish Lifecycle," by Rabbi Samuel Kieffer. In addition, we are grateful to the Rabbinical Assembly for granting permission to use portions from "This is My Beloved, This is My Friend: A Rabbinic Letter on Intimate Relations," by Rabbi Elliot N. Dorff for the Commission on Human Sexuality. This publication served as a foundation for much of our discussion about sexuality. Finally, thank you to USY's Education Coordinator, Amy Dorsch, for her work on each of the preliminary drafts. Amy's creativity and talent brought a life to the sourcebook through its activities and questions. I have enjoyed having Amy as my chevruta and friend for this project.

It is with great appreciation that we acknowledge the USY family of readers whose talents and suggestions helped to shape this book—Rabbi Paul Drazen, Dr. Shira Epstein, Jonathan S. Greenberg, Jules A. Gutin, David Srebnick and Gila Hadani Ward.

I am grateful to my USY colleagues at the United Synagogue of Conservative Judaism who have all been extremely encouraging throughout the entire process. Additionally, I am most grateful to my husband, Adam Monaco, and our sweet son, Avi Benjamin. May Avi grow up in a world that is tolerant and respectful and someday find himself happily in many healthy relationships.

Karen L. Stein
December, 2009/ Kislev, 5770

JEWISH WOMEN INTERNATIONAL

December 2009

Dear Friends,

We are thrilled by the opportunity to be collaborating with USY on this very important project. By placing this Sourcebook in the hands of hundreds of USY leaders, and potentially reaching thousands of USY members, JWI is one step further in its goal to place core curriculum on healthy relationships inside our Jewish educational organizations. JWI, and its 75,000 members and supporters applaud USY and the USCJ for wholeheartedly embracing this vision. We would like to thank in particular, Rabbi Jerome Epstein, Rabbi Paul Drazen, Jules Gutin and Karen Stein for their leadership and commitment to this initiative.

Deborah Rosenbloom, JWI's director of programs, directed, authored and oversaw this project from its inception to its conclusion. Additional thanks go to a number of young women who contributed to the Sourcebook, Rella Kaplowitz, a former JWI program staffer who wrote its first draft, Hannah Helfman, a 2009 summer intern, and Lila Z. Rosenbloom, former Seaboard Region, USY Executive/Israeli Affairs, Vice President. JWI also thanks The Hadassah Foundation, the Joseph and Harvey Meyerhoff Family Foundation, the Toby and Nataly Ritter Family Foundation, and JWI's Mahoning Valley Chapter in Youngstown, Ohio for their generous support and commitment to the well-being of Jewish teens.

Today's teens are bombarded with confusing messages about relationships, sexuality, aggression, and violence. One-third of teens report experiencing physical, verbal and/or emotional abuse and teens also report that bullying, whether face-to-face or via technology, is at its highest levels ever. Jewish values supporting respect, gender equality, leadership, and self-esteem can serve as a much needed antidote to the difficult challenges of being a teenager in the 21st century.

JWI is proud to provide resources that combat and challenge today's norms through a Jewish lens, with text studies, interactive exercises, and strong messaging. In 2005, JWI created the first national Jewish educational program to address dating abuse, When Push Comes to Shove…It's No Longer Love!® Since then JWI has released a succession of healthy relationship programs for Jewish teens. Strong Girls: A Conversation on Dating, Friendship and Self-Esteem; Good Guys: Partnership & Positive Masculinity, and others in the series have reached thousands of teens nationwide and abroad.

It is our hope that teens throughout USY's 17 regions and 400 local chapters are able to benefit from this Sourcebook and our other healthy relationships programs and resources. We urge every Conservative synagogue to follow the lead of USY and make this issue a priority within its own congregation. With your help, we can make our world a safer place for all our teens.

Sincerely,

Lori Weinstein
Executive Director

Susan W. Turnbull
Chair, Board of Trustees

Guide To Jewish Texts

Torah/Five Books of Moses:
Beresheit- Genesis
Shmot- Exodus
Vayikra- Leviticus
Bamidbar- Numbers
D'varim- Deuteronomy

Nevi'im/Prophets
Shoftim- Judges
Shmuel I and II – Samuel I and II
Yeshaya- Isaiah
Yirmiyahu- Jeremiah
Yehezkel- Ezekiel
Hoshea- Hosea

K'tuvim/Writings
Tehilim- Psalms
Mishlei- Proverbs
Ruth- Ruth
Shir HaShirim- Song of Songs
Kohelet- Ecclesiastes
Pirkei Avot- Ethics of the Sages
Rabbah- Midrash on that particular book

Part One

וְאָהַבְתָּ לְרֵעֲךָ כָּמוֹךָ

LOVE YOUR neighBOR, LOVE YOURSELF

Building Healthy Relationships

In this section we will begin our exploration of healthy relationships, discussing Jewish values and texts that support creating and maintaining these relationships. We will think about the different communities to which we belong, our responsibility for other people and to ourselves, and the importance of friendship, especially as a basis for an intimate relationship.

Judaism places a great deal of emphasis on encouraging healthy relationships with our friends, partners, siblings, parents, and members of our communities. We learn this from the many Jewish texts teaching ways we should and should not interact with people. This chapter will explore some of those texts and values and provide you with some tools to think about your own relationships. By deepening our own understanding of relationships, we will each be better equipped to be a good friend, partner, and community member.

יז לֹא-תִשְׂנָא אֶת-אָחִיךָ, בִּלְבָבֶךָ; הוֹכֵחַ תּוֹכִיחַ אֶת-עֲמִיתֶךָ, וְלֹא-תִשָּׂא עָלָיו חֵטְא.

17 You shall not hate your kinsman in your heart. Reprove your neighbor, but incur no guilt because of him.

יח לֹא-תִקֹּם וְלֹא-תִטֹּר אֶת-בְּנֵי עַמֶּךָ, וְאָהַבְתָּ לְרֵעֲךָ כָּמוֹךָ: אֲנִי, יְהוָה.

18 You shall not take vengeance or bear a grudge against your kinsfolk. **Love your neighbor as yourself**: I am the Lord

(Vayikra 19: 17-18)

What does it mean to "love yourself?"
I love myself by _____.
What does v'ahavta l'rayecha kamocha mean to you?

"Love your neighbor" is the common translation of this phrase, but it can also be translated "Be as loving to your neighbor as you would to yourself." ***Does this change the meaning at all?*** There can be two ways to interpret the translation of this text: "Love your neighbor as you would love yourself" and "love your neighbor as you would want to be loved." ***How do you interpret this text? Do you have to love yourself before you can learn to be loving to your neighbor? How can you respect others if you don't cherish who you are?***

לג וְכִי-יָגוּר אִתְּךָ גֵּר, בְּאַרְצְכֶם--לֹא תוֹנוּ, אֹתוֹ.

33 When a stranger resides with you in your land, you shall not wrong him..

לד כְּאֶזְרָח מִכֶּם יִהְיֶה לָכֶם הַגֵּר הַגָּר אִתְּכֶם, וְאָהַבְתָּ לוֹ כָּמוֹךָ--כִּי-גֵרִים הֱיִיתֶם, בְּאֶרֶץ מִצְרָיִם: אֲנִי, יְהוָה אֱלֹהֵיכֶם.

34 The stranger who resides with you shall be to you as one of your citizens; **you shall love him as yourself,** for you were strangers in the land of Egypt: I am the Lord your God.

(Vayikra 19:33-34)

We see that the Rabbis who studied the Talmud centuries later recognized the importance of this Leviticus verse through the stories they told:

שוב מעשה בנכרי אחד שבא לפני שמאי, אמר לו: גיירני על מנת שתלמדני כל התורה כולה כשאני עומד על רגל אחת. דחפו באמת הבנין שבידו. בא לפני הלל, גייריה. אמר לו: דעלך סני לחברך לא תעביד - זו היא כל התורה כולה, ואידך - פירושה הוא, זיל גמור

There is a story told of a man who wanted to learn everything about the Torah. The man went up to Rabbi Shammai and said, "Can you teach me the Torah while I stand on one foot?" Rabbi Shammai looked at him and laughed. "You crazy fool! I can not teach you the entire Torah in such a short of time." The man walked away and soon came upon Rabbi Hillel. Again, he asked the same questions, "Can you teach me the Torah while I stand one foot?" Rabbi Hillel thought for just a moment and then replied, "What is hateful to you, do not do unto your neighbor. This is the entire Torah; all the rest is commentary."

(Talmud Shabbat 31a)

עַל שְׁלשָׁה דְבָרִים הָעוֹלָם עוֹמֵד, עַל הַתּוֹרָה וְעַל הָעֲבוֹדָה וְעַל גְּמִילוּת חֲסָדִים
On three things the world is sustained: On the Torah, on worship, and on acts of loving kindness.
(Pirkei Avot 1:2)

What is an "act of loving kindness?"
Acts of loving kindness are more, much more than acts of charity – they connect us directly to people and help us create relationships with people. Interestingly, both people in a relationship benefit from the act of loving kindness – these are truly acts of active 'friendship.'

An example of an act of loving kindness I have done or know makes a difference is:

_____

_____

_____

This text tells us that the rabbis thought that doing good things for others is as important as learning Torah and worship in supporting the existence of the world.

Do you agree or disagree that these three constructs are the pillars of the world? Do you think any do not belong, or that any are missing?

Activity: Al Shlosha D'varim:

Draw a globe on top of the three pillars according to *Pirkei Avot*. If you could change one of the pillars, which would it be? What would you replace it with? Draw this new globe with new pillars.

Now think about what sustains you and your world. What are the three pillars of your world?

Draw a globe supported by your three pillars.

Loving Your Fellow Person- the Importance of Relationships

Rabbi Moshe Leib [of Sassov, a late 18th-century Ukrainian Hasidic master] told this story: "How to love men [i.e., other persons] is something I learned from a peasant. He was sitting in an inn with other peasants, drinking. For a long time he was as silent as all the rest, but when he was moved by wine, he asked one of the men seated beside him, 'Tell me, do you love me or don't you love me?'

"The other peasant replied, 'I love you very much'.

"But the first peasant replied, 'You say that you love me, but you do not know what I need. If you really loved me, you would know.'

"The other had not a word to say to this, and the peasant who had put the question fell silent again.

"But I understood. To know the needs of men and to bear the burden of their sorrow-- that is the true love of men."

-- Martin Buber (1878-1965), a well known author and Jewish thinker (can be found in *Tales of the Hasidim*, vol. 2: The Later Masters, Schocken Books.)

Chesed Shel Emet—The Truest Act of Kindness

Chesed Shel Emet - "the truest act of kindness" is the act of preparing the dead body for burial. Of all acts of chesed one can perform for another, it is considered the only truly selfless act, since there is no possibility that the other person can repay the kindness. Traditionally, a Jewish burial society called a *Chevra Kadisha* —"Holy Society"— performs the *chesed shel emet* to meet the obligation to care for the dead on behalf of the community In death, everyone becomes equal, and all, rich or poor, are prepared for burial in exactly the same way.

Do we only do acts of kindness in order to be paid back? Do you expect a reward when you do nice things for others?

Why would caring for the dead be considered such a true chesed? Would you want to be member of a Chevre Kadisha and perform the sacred deeds of chesed shel emet?

Activity: Practice Random Acts of Kindness

What do you think is the value of performing a random act of loving kindness? Why?

Do you think it is harder or easier to be kind to a stranger than to a family member? Why? How about to a friend? Why

You've probably seen the bumper sticker that says: "Do a Random Act of Kindness Today".

What would your bumper sticker about kindness say? Design it here:

The Talmud teaches: "The Torah begins with an act of kindness, and ends with an act of kindness. It begins with an act of kindness, for it says, God made garments of skin for Adam and his wife and clothed them (Bereishit 3:21). And it ends with an act of kindness, for it says, "He buried Moses in the valley." (Dvarim 34:6; Sotah 14a)

Chapter One
we're all in this together · community

You are part of a larger network of others. You belong to a community.
Let's start with the concept of being part of a community:

כל ישראל ערבים זה בזה   All Israel is responsible for one another.

(Talmud, Shavuot 39a)

What does it mean to be part of a community? How do you show you are responsible for others? Can you be responsible for someone whom you do not know?

אִם אֵין אֲנִי לִי, מִי לִי.   "If I am not for myself, who will be for me?
וּכְשֶׁאֲנִי לְעַצְמִי, מָה אֲנִי.   If I am only for myself, what am I?
וְאִם לֹא עַכְשָׁיו, אֵימָתַי.   And if not now, when?"

(Pirkei Avot 1:14)

Does this text seem contradictory? How can you be both for yourself and be for others? How does this text recognize not only the uniqueness of the individual, but also the connection and responsibility each individual has to others?

These two texts assume that all of us are connected to one another – by being part of the Jewish community. As part of that community, we are responsible for every other person in that community. As a part of the *Jewish* community, we share certain values, such as the importance of the Torah in guiding our lives, the concept that there is one God, the importance of education, and of family, as well as holidays, prayers, a country, a history, and more.

Think of 3 things we share as members of the Jewish community:

1.	
2.	
3.	

We get strength and support from being part of a community and in turn we are able to support and strengthen our community. Think for example about the minyan, the group of ten adults required for a prayer service. It is preferable for us to pray as part of a minyan – praying together is one way in which we show our support for our community. Certain prayers, like the Kaddish, can only be said if a minyan is present. Many mourners, for example, will seek out minyan during this time, specifically so they can recite the Mourner's Kaddish. They are looking for the support of being with other members of their community.

Why do you think that it is important to pray as part of a community? Does that strengthen our connections to each other? How?

What do you think the value is of praying in a minyan during the time of mourning? How does this requirement strengthen our connections to each other?

What are benefits to being part of a community?

We are responsible for each other and we are part of a community because of our connections to each other. Connection can mean different things to different people. Think about a person you feel a connection to in your life:

I feel that I am connected to _____

because _____

Activity: We are Family!
How closely are we all connected in the Jewish world?

Jew-o-graphy: It's a very small Jewish world. Who are you connected to? Think of three last names in your family (aunts, uncles, maiden names, married names) and write them here:

| |
| |
| |
| |

Ask your friends if anyone has any of the same names in their family—you may be surprised! The world is a very narrow bridge- we're all connected or related!

But am I connected to everyone in the same way?

וְאִם יִתְקְפוֹ הָאֶחָד הַשְּׁנַיִם יַעַמְדוּ נֶגְדּוֹ
וְהַחוּט הַמְשֻׁלָּשׁ לֹא בִמְהֵרָה יִנָּתֵק

"And if a [person] prevail against him that is alone, two shall withstand him; and a threefold cord is not quickly broken."
(Kohelet 4:12)

 Think of "connections" like the cord described in the text above from Kohelet or chains that link people together. These chains can be made out of different types of material. For example, maybe you are connected to another person in your school by a paper chain—you don't know him or her very well, so the chain could be torn very easily, or damaged by water or fire. That is a weak connection.

Now think of a friend of yours—not your best friend, but someone you like to hang out with. The chain between you and your friend is stronger, perhaps made of plastic. It's stronger than paper, but can still be broken pretty easily.

Now think about someone with whom you are very close—it might be a friend, a sibling, or a parent. Your chain is made of something strong and durable like metal. It can withstand water, fire and physical force. Even if someone tried to pull you apart, you would stay connected to each other. We're stronger when supported by others.

How do we create these chains?

How do we strengthen our chains?

What things do we do that might weaken the chains?

Activity: Lean on Me!

In general, human beings rely on each other. Try this activity to demonstrate the universal need for support.

Try leaning to one side as far as possible before you lose your balance. Now find another person and have him or her stand shoulder-to-shoulder with you and lean in until you almost lose your balance. Keep adding more people until the entire group has formed a leaning line.

The more people that are added to the leaning line, the more the line will be able to withstand the lean. **How can you apply this to community?**

Do you think the concept of connection is important in Jewish thought? Why or why not?

Jewish texts can help explain how human beings are meant to rely on one another. The challenges we face may throw us off balance but there will always be someone to "lean on" in the Jewish community.

In Pirkei Avot 2:5, we learn that Hillel said:

אַל תִּפְרוֹשׁ מִן הַצִּבּוּר "Do not separate yourself from the community."

Hillel uses a negative statement, telling us not to do something. Why do you think Hillel doesn't use the positive statement telling us to "be part of a community?"

Activity: What communities do you belong to?

Most people belong to a variety of communities. For example, your circle of friends is your community as well as your school, camp friends, baseball team, USY chapter or your neighborhood. What communities do you belong to?

What shared values do you have with each of these groups? What makes them communities?

Activity: Everyone Wants a Piece of the Pie

Using the communities that you named above, create a "pie" showing how much time you spend with each group every week. If you spend a lot of time with a group, draw a big slice. If you spend only a little time with a group, draw a smaller slice. You may spend summers with one group, such as your friends from Wheels, and then not see them the rest of the year. Still, that would get a large slice since that is a large chunk of time. Label each slice with the name of the community.

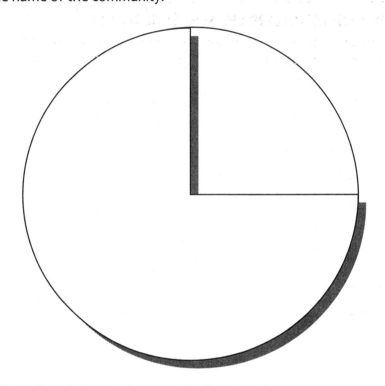

1. *Are you spending a lot of time with one particular group?*
2. *Why do you spend more time with that group as opposed to another?*
3. *Can you consider yourself a member of a community if you don't put time into it?*
4. *Do you like spending a lot of time with that group? Why or why not?*
5. *Is there a group you don't spend a lot of time with, but want to? Why or why not?*
6. *Do you ever feel torn between two groups, like you have to choose one or the other?*
7. *What obligations do you have if you belong to a community?*
8. *People seek out communities for many reasons. Why have you chosen these communities?*

Fill in some reasons here:

Another way to do this exercise is to divide the pie into 24 hours and figure out how much time you spend with these communities on a daily basis.

Activity: A Different Kind of Human Pyramid

Draw out a "people pyramid," a pyramid divided into sections. Write the names of significant people in your life, beginning with the foundation and moving upward in relationship significance. Which people in your life are the foundation of your person, the base that keeps you firmly grounded, which are the middle row of importance and finally the top? How lucky you are to have so many people (although at different levels of significance) in your life!

We are fortunate to belong to many different communities.

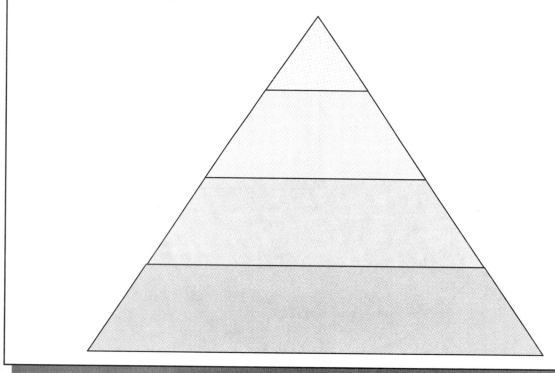

Connecting On-Line

A lot of teens spend a great deal of time interacting online - Facebook® , MySpace®, chatrooms, etc., have replaced much of the time that we spend face to face with friends and neighbors. A false sense of intimacy and closeness can quickly develop in online relationships and teens often feel that they are truly connected to their online friends.

Is there such a thing as an 'online community'? If yes, how would you define it? How do you become a member of it? If no, why not?

How do you relate differently to people online than you do face to face?

What type of things do you share or say online that you would not share or say to people in person?

Relationships and Mitzvot

The word 'relationship' is often used to describe our connection with one special person – for example you've probably been asked the question: "Are you in a relationship?," meaning, are you dating anyone, are you 'seeing' anyone? In Judaism however, the concept of being in a relationship is much broader – in fact, everything we do, every aspect of our lives, is seen as being part of a relationship. We know this because many of the 613 mitzvot commanded in the Torah involve a relationship.

There are four categories to these relationships. They are the relationship between:

- a person and God (these are called *bein adam l'makom* — בֵּין אָדָם לְמָקוֹם);
- a person and a friend (these are called *bein adam l'chavero* — בֵּין אָדָם לַחֲבֵרוֹ);
- a person and him or herself (*bein adam l'atzmo* — בֵּין אָדָם לְעַצְמוֹ)

Mitzvot which are *bein adam l'makom* between a person and God—include putting *tzitzit* (fringes) on the corners of clothing (Bamidbar 15:38) and keeping kosher (D'varim 14:3-22). Mitzvot which are b*ein adam l'chavero*—between two people—include giving *tzedakah* (D'varim 15:7) and not bearing a grudge (Vayikra 19:18). Mitzvot which are between a person and himself—help us take care of ourselves. Examples include the commandment not to be involved with self destructive behavior on ourselves, not to listen to gossip (Vayikra 19:16), and taking care our bodies (Vayikra Rabbah 34:3).

Let's look at the phrase '*bein adam l'Makom*'. Why is the word '*Makom*' used for God? In Hebrew, there are a number of different names by which we refer to God. One of those names is "*HaMakom,*" which literally means "the place" or "the space." According to Jewish philosopher Martin Buber, God's presence, the *shechinah*, is not found in people, but in the 'space' between people. The *shechinah* resides in the relationships people have with each other. It is our responsibility to ensure that the *shechinah* will rest in our relationships.

Now let's think about the term '*bein adam l'chavero*'—mitzvot between two people. The word *chaver* means friend. Does this mean that these mitzvot only apply to our relationships with friends? What do you think? How else can friend be defined? Even if we use the word *chavero* very loosely, does it imply that these mitzvot only apply to people with whom we have a pre-existing relationship?

Activity: Dividing Your Time

Consider how you spend your time on an average day. Divide your average day according to how much of your time is dedicated to each of the three types of relationships.

List examples of mitzvot or general actions you do that would fall under each relationship.
Do you take time for God? For yourself? For friends and family? In what ways?

Bein Adam L'chavero: My Friends
1.
2.
3.
4.

Bein Adam L'Makom: Me and My G-O-D
1.
2.
3.
4.

Bein Adam L'atzmo: Me, Myself and I
1.
2.
3.
4.

Activity: Match The Mitzvah

While we are commanded to perform most mitzvot without knowing what the reward will be for performing them, the Torah tells us that our lives will be lengthened if we perform three specific *mitzvot*. **See if you can identify which relationship of mitzvot each of the following texts fall into:**

A: Between a Person and God (Bein Adam L'Makom);
B. Between a Person and a Friend (Bein Adam L'Chavero)
C. Between a Person and Him or Herself (Bein Adam L'Atzmo)

How do these categories shed light on the importance of our relationships?

What do you think these commandments have in common?

Why do you feel these are these important *mitzvot*?

MITZVAH	RELATIONSHIP
כַּבֵּד אֶת־אָבִיךָ וְאֶת־אִמֶּךָ לְמַעַן יַאֲרִכוּן יָמֶיךָ עַל הָאֲדָמָה אֲשֶׁר־יְהֹוָה אֱלֹהֶיךָ נֹתֵן לָךְ: Honor your father and your mother; that your days may be long upon the land which the Lord your God gives you. (Shmot 20:12)	
לֹא־יִהְיֶה לְךָ בְּכִיסְךָ אֶבֶן וָאָבֶן גְּדוֹלָה וּקְטַנָּה: You shall not have in your bag different weights, a large and a small. (i.e. to be honest in our business dealings) (D'varim 25:13)	
וּכְתַבְתָּם עַל־מְזוּזוֹת בֵּיתֶךָ וּבִשְׁעָרֶיךָ: And you shall write them upon the door posts of your house, and upon your gates; (D'varim 11:20)	
וַיִּבְרָא אֱלֹהִים אֶת-הָאָדָם בְּצַלְמוֹ, בְּצֶלֶם אֱלֹהִים בָּרָא אֹתוֹ : זָכָר וּנְקֵבָה, בָּרָא אֹתָם. And God created man in His own image, in the image of God created He him; male and female created He them. (Bereishit 1:27)	

Let's look at the most commonly known *mitzvot*, the Ten Commandments or *Aseret Ha'Dibrot*: Shmot: 20:2-14. The Ten Commandments are like a "Top 10 Rules to Live By" and involve all four relationship types:

1. I the Lord am your God who brought you out of the land of Egypt, the house of bondage:

2. You shall have no other gods besides Me. You shall not make for yourself a sculpture image, or any likeness of what is in the heavens above, or on the earth below, or in the waters under the earth. You shall not bow down to them or serve them. For I ....

3. You shall not swear falsely by the name of the Lord your God

4. Remember the Sabbath day and keep it holy

5. Honor your father and your mother, that you may long endure on the land....

6. You shall not murder

7. You shall not commit adultery

8. You shall not steal

9. You shall not bear false witness against your neighbor

10. You shall not covet your neighbor's house: you shall not covet your neighbor's wife, or his male or female slave, or his ox or his donkey, or anything that is your neighbor's.

Activity: Divide the Big Ten into Three

Into which relationships (categories)of *mitzvot* do the Ten Commandments fall?

Bein Adam L'chavero: My Friends and Me	Bein Adam L'makom: Me and My G-O-D	Bein Adam L'atzmo: Me, Myself and I

Many scholars find that the first five commandments are between a person and God and the second five are between people. But look at the commandment to honor one's parents:

יא כַּבֵּד אֶת-אָבִיךָ, וְאֶת-אִמֶּךָ--לְמַעַן, 11 Honor your father and your mother, that you
יַאֲרִכוּן יָמֶיךָ, עַל הָאֲדָמָה, אֲשֶׁר-יְהוָה may long endure on the land.
אֱלֹהֶיךָ נֹתֵן לָךְ.

(Shmot 20:11)

- *Do you agree that this is a commandment between a person and God?*
- *Why would it make sense for this commandment to be between a person and God?*
- *What do God and parents share in common?*
- *Do you think this is a difficult commandment to keep? What challenges or obstacles stand in the way?*

On the other hand, perhaps this commandment really falls into the second category and in that case, six of the Ten Commandments are really between a person and a fellow person. What would that tell us about the importance of human relationships? Does this mean that our relationships with people are at least as important as our relationship with God?

Now let's look at the Tenth Commandment, not to covet our neighbor's property.
Why do you think the admonition not to 'covet' is limited to our neighbor?

יג לֹא תַחְמֹד, בֵּית רֵעֶךָ ; לֹא-תַחְמֹד אֵשֶׁת 13 You shall not covet your neighbor's house: you
רֵעֶךָ, וְעַבְדּוֹ וַאֲמָתוֹ וְשׁוֹרוֹ וַחֲמֹרוֹ, וְכֹל, אֲשֶׁר shall not covet your neighbor's wife, or his male or
לְרֵעֶךָ. female slave, or his ox or his donkey, or anything
that is your neighbor's.

(Shmot 20:13)

- *Is it different if we covet or are jealous of our neighbor's property and wealth as opposed to a stranger's wealth? How?*
- *How would being jealous of someone within our community affect our community?*

For further thought: What about total strangers? What are our obligations toward them?

> Repentance and forgiveness on Yom Kippur are only for those sins between a person and God like eating something forbidden, or engaging in forbidden activities, and the like. But sins between a person and his friend like hurting, cursing or stealing from a friend, he will not be forgiven by God until he reconciles with his friend.
> (Mishneh Torah L'HaRambam, Hilchot Teshuva, 2:9)

What does this text tell us about the importance of our person-to-person relationships?

One might think that the most significant relationship is between and person and God, but the Rambam, Maimonides, tells us this is not the case. In fact, not only must a person resolve conflict with friends, he or she has to do that before God will absolve any sins. From this we learn that not only are our relationships with others highly significant and valued in Judaism, they make take precedence over our relationship with God. Why do you think this is the case?

Chapter Two
Friendship

א שִׁיר הַמַּעֲלוֹת, לְדָוִד: 1 A Song of Ascents; of David.

הִנֵּה מַה-טּוֹב, וּמַה-נָּעִים — שֶׁבֶת אַחִים גַּם-יָחַד.   How good it is, and how pleasant, when brethren dwell in harmony.

If we translate the text literally, it says: "How good and how pleasant it is – when brothers sit <u>also</u> together."

- *Do you think this verse is only referring to siblings? Who else might be sitting together?*
- *Look at the underlined word. What does the word "also" add to the meaning?*

Siblings are related by default, but it doesn't mean they have a good relationship. The word 'also' means that is it nice and pleasant for anyone connected through a specific relationship, including siblings, to sit together in harmony.

- *In this age of technology, "sitting together" might not mean physically sitting next to each other. How do technologies like the internet and cell phones connect people? What are some ways technology also keeps people apart?*
- *In what ways does technology make interaction easier or harder?*
- *How would you describe relationships through which you connect mostly via technology?*

A Story of Brotherly Love

Once there were two brothers who inherited a farm. They worked the farm together for years in brotherly love. After a time, one of them found a wife, so the brothers divided up the farm. The married one built a new house and lived with his wife, while the other brother lived by himself in the old building. The brothers continued to work their farms and they flourished and made a lot of money.

The one who had a wife eventually had some children—a large family, ten children. The other brother was still looking for a wife; he was alone.

One day, the brother who was alone thought to himself: "I've got that whole farm and all that money, but I only have myself to take care of. My brother has the same amount as me, but he has twelve mouths to feed." So in the middle of the night he took some bundles of wheat, climbed up the hill that separated the two farms, and put the wheat in his brother's silo.

Azriel Eisenberg, "Brotherly Love" in Jerusalem Eternal (New York: Board of Jewish Education Inc., 1971), p.51-52 used with permission in Rejoice With Jerusalem by Jules Gutin, 1983.

One night the married brother was thinking to himself, "You know, I've got ten kids, I've got a wife. My world is rich. But my brother, he's all alone. What does he have? All he has is his wheat." So, in the middle of the night, he took a bundle of wheat, climbed the hill, and carried it to his brother's silo.

Back and forth each of the brothers went. Every night each one would climb the hill, pass by to the other side and put wheat in the other's silo. And the next morning each one always wondered, "Why do I have the same amount of wheat?"

One night, while they were passing by to bring the other their bundles of wheat, the two brothers met at the top of the hill. And immediately they understood what had been happening. They fell into each other's arms, hugging in love for each other.

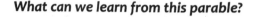

It is on that site that the Almighty chose to build the Holy Temple.

What can we learn from this parable?

Why would God choose to build the Temple on this site? What does this teach us?

The love of the brothers in this story is an example of *ahavat chinam*—love without a price, or love that is not dependent on receiving anything in return—love just because. Relationships that are filled with *ahavat chinam* are most desirable by God. In contrast, the second Temple was destroyed because of *sin'at chinam*—baseless hatred, or hating someone for no reason.

The brothers in this story each gave up a lot to make sure the other was happy.
Do you think a friend should have to give something up for a friendship? How much is too much?

The brothers in this story each chose to sacrifice without being asked or forced. Relationships are complicated and require compromise and sometimes sacrifice. Compromising is part of a healthy relationship but there should be boundaries about what we compromise.

1. *How does it make you feel when you make a compromise for a friend?*
2. *How do you decide if this is the right thing to do?*
3. *What are the boundaries between acts of friendship and being used?*
4. *Go back to the pie you made earlier. Were you represented on the pie?*

How do you balance your personal commitments and the needs of your friends? What are commitments that are appropriate between friends? What is the difference between having a friendship that includes emotional commitments and having friendships that consist mostly of driving your friends on their errands? Do you have any friendships that lack an emotional commitment? How much do you value those friendships? How do they make you feel?

Compromise and Sacrifice:
What is the difference between making a compromise for a friend and making a sacrifice? Can you think of a personal example of each? When is it okay to sacrifice for a friend?

What do you look for in a friend?

_____ _____ _____

_____ _____ _____

What can challenge or destroy a friendship?

_____ _____ _____

_____ _____ _____

What makes **you** a good friend?

_____ _____ _____

_____ _____ _____

What qualities do you offer as a friend?

_____ _____ _____

_____ _____

Would you want yourself as a friend?

Acquire For Yourself a Friend

עֲשֵׂה לְךָ רַב, וּקְנֵה לְךָ חָבֵר,
וֶהֱוֵי דָן אֶת כָּל הָאָדָם לְכַף זְכוּת:

Find for yourself a teacher, acquire for yourself a friend, and judge every person favorably.

(Pirkei Avot 1:6)

What does it mean to "acquire" a friend?

How is that different than "having" a friend?

Friendship doesn't just happen. It takes time and effort to establish and maintain relationships. Similar to translating *"v'ahavta l'rayecha kamocha"* as "be loving to your neighbor," using the word "acquire," makes friendship action oriented—you have to work for it.

Why are these three ideas stated together? What do finding a teacher, acquiring a friend and judging every person favorably have to do with each other?

This statement highlights three critical necessities in life. The first is having a mentor—someone to learn from, and to help you grow and achieve. The second is a friend—someone to support you as you strive to new and greater heights and accomplish your goals. The third is a positive outlook on life—to have the ability to be an optimist in all aspects of life, to see things in a good light, even when life throws you curveballs.

What else does it take to be a good friend?

> "The only way to have a friend is to be one."
> Ralph Waldo Emerson

What do you think Emerson is saying here? Do you agree or disagree?

People often say that they have many acquaintances, but there are few people who have more than one or two close friends. How many close friends do you have? How do we secure a friend? What is the nature of true friendship? What are the ethical demands that friendship makes upon us? What are the rewards in having friends?

The Hebrew word **chaver** is often used in the rabbinic writings to mean a friend. But the word chaver has many other connotations as well, including: colleague, comrade, study partner, associate, partner, companion, and fellow. It should therefore come as no surprise that the same Hebrew word for friend, chaver, is also used for members of groups that share common goals and responsibilities.

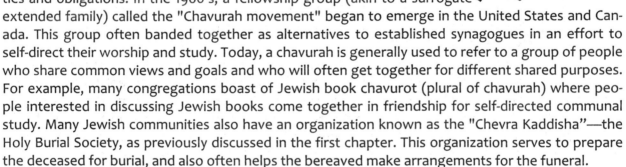

You may have heard of the word **chavurah.** The Talmudic rabbis were members of an association called a chavurah which shared certain responsibilities and obligations. In the 1960's, a fellowship group (akin to a surrogate extended family) called the "Chavurah movement" began to emerge in the United States and Canada. This group often banded together as alternatives to established synagogues in an effort to self-direct their worship and study. Today, a chavurah is generally used to refer to a group of people who share common views and goals and who will often get together for different shared purposes. For example, many congregations boast of Jewish book chavurot (plural of chavurah) where people interested in discussing Jewish books come together in friendship for self-directed communal study. Many Jewish communities also have an organization known as the "Chevra Kaddisha"—the Holy Burial Society, as previously discussed in the first chapter. This organization serves to prepare the deceased for burial, and also often helps the bereaved make arrangements for the funeral.

Another Hebrew word for friend is **re'eh.** It is interesting that in the fifth of the seven wedding blessings, both husband and wife are referred to as **re'im ahuvim** -- best friends or loving companions. What do you think this suggests about the way in which the rabbis envisioned the relationship of a husband and his wife? We will discuss this further in the chapter on Marriage.

As teenagers in High School, no doubt you are beginning to feel the pressures of school life, especially in thinking about gaining entrance into the college or occupation of your choice. Having a close friend or two can go a long way in helping to alleviate some of the stresses and frustrations often encountered in the life of a teenager.

One Talmudic rabbi offered this statement as a description of friendship between students: **'Acquire a friend."** (Pirkei Avot 1:6) How? This teaches that a person should acquire a friend. He should eat with him, read with him, study with him, sleep in the same house with him, and reveal his secrets to him - the secrets of the Torah (i.e., methods of reasoning) and the secrets of worldly things. (Avot d'Rabbi Natan, 8)

The degree of intimacy in the above description is nothing short of amazing. Friends are obligated to share not only their intellectual gifts, but their physical surroundings as well.

Why do you think friends should eat and sleep together? Do you think that this is a reasonable requirement today?

Do you feel that friends should be sharing secrets with each other? Why or why not? Was there ever a time when you felt you needed to share a secret with a friend? Are there secrets that you would not feel comfortable sharing, even with your best friend? Why?

Following are some other examples of what Jewish writers have said about friendship and making friends. After reading them, spend some time discussing the questions and exercises that follow:

The Value of Friendship

A rich man had ten sons. He swore to them that when his time came to die he would leave each of them one hundred dinars. As time went by, however, he lost part of his money, and all that remained was nine hundred and fifty dinars. So he gave a hundred dinars apiece to each of his nine elder sons. To his youngest son he said: "I have only fifty dinars left, and I must put aside thirty of them for burial expenses. I can leave you only twenty. But I have ten companions, whom I will give to you, and they are better than a thousand dinars."

The man told his friends about his youngest son, and soon afterward he died and was buried. The nine sons went their ways, and the youngest son gradually spent the few dinars that had been left to him. When he had only one left, he decided to spend it on a feast for his father's ten friends. They ate and drank with him, and said to one another, "He is the only one of all the brothers who still cares for us. Let us show him kindness in return for his luridness." So they each gave him a cow and money. The cows gave birth and he sold them, and he used his money to start a business. God blessed him and made him richer than his father. Then he said, "Indeed, my father said that friends are better than all the money in the world."

(Legend in An Elegant Composition Concerning Relief After Adversity, compiled by Nissim ben Jacob ben Nissim, New Haven, 1977).

There were two close friends who had been parted by war so that they lived in different kingdoms. Once one of them came to visit his friend, and because he came from the city of the king's enemy, he was imprisoned and sentenced to be executed as a spy. No amount of pleas would save him, so he begged the king for one kindness. "Your majesty," he said, "let me have just one month to return to my land and put my affairs in order so my family will be cared for after my death. At the end of the month I will return to pay the penalty." "How can I believe you will return?" answered the king. "What security can you offer?" "My friend will be my security," said the man. "He will pay for my life with his if I do not return." The king called in the man's friend, and to his amazement, the friend agreed to the conditions.

On the last day of the month, the sun was setting, and the man had not yet returned. The king ordered his friend killed in his stead. As the sword was about to descend, the man returned and quickly placed the sword on his own neck. But his friend stopped him. "Let me die for you," he pleaded. The king was deeply moved. He ordered the sword taken away and pardoned both of them. "Since there is such great love and friendship between the two of you," he said, "I entreat you to let me join you as a third." And from that day on they became the king's companions. And it was in this spirit that our sages of blessed memory said, "Get yourself a companion."

(Legend in Beit HaMidrash, Adolf Jellinek)

Beit Ha-Midrash is a six-volume anthology of little-known midrashim and apocryphal writings edited in the mid-nineteenth century by Adolph Jellinek.

- *What must one do to keep a friendship going strong? Why do you believe that some friendships dissolve while others are longer lasting? What makes for a longer lasting one?*
- *Think about a friend who is very dear to you. How did your friendship start?*
- *Why are you still friends with that person?*
- *What steps do you take to maintain that relationship?*
- *What do you value in that friend?*
- *What characteristics of friendship does this text tell us about?*

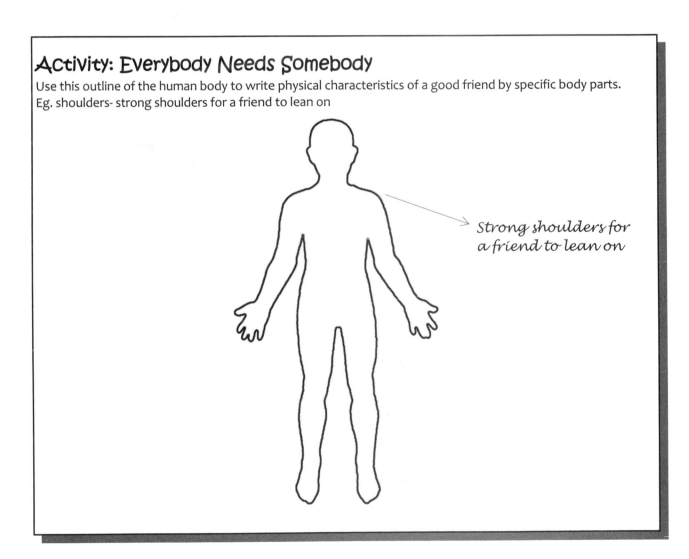

Activity: Everybody Needs Somebody
Use this outline of the human body to write physical characteristics of a good friend by specific body parts. Eg. shoulders- strong shoulders for a friend to lean on

Strong shoulders for a friend to lean on

Activity: Are you a good friend?

Try a little friendship self-evaluation test!

When a friend calls to complain or is upset about something, do you actively listen? Do you offer to hang out with him/her?

Everyone's going to a big party this weekend. Your friend isn't allowed to go and asks if you'll go with him/her to a movie. Do you go with him/her

Your friend is home sick and doesn't ask you for the day's homework but do you collect it for her/him anyway

Your friend is having her braces removed and asks you to go with her. You really don't want to. Do you go?

Your friend is being teased on a daily basis by one of your other friends. Do you stand up for her/him and say something?

Make a list of qualities you look for in a friend. Write the name of someone you know that exhibits these qualities.

One aspect of friendship is the support we can receive from others, and in turn, the support we can give to our friends.

ט טוֹבִים הַשְּׁנַיִם, מִן-הָאֶחָד : אֲשֶׁר יֶשׁ-לָהֶם שָׂכָר טוֹב, בַּעֲמָלָם.

9 Two are better than one because they have a good reward for their labor.

י כִּי אִם-יִפֹּלוּ, הָאֶחָד יָקִים אֶת-חֲבֵרוֹ ; וְאִילוֹ, הָאֶחָד שֶׁיִּפּוֹל, וְאֵין שֵׁנִי, לַהֲקִימוֹ.

10 For if they fall, the one will lift up his fellow; but woe to him that is alone when he falls, for he has not another to help him up.

(Kohelet, 4:9-10)

This text talks about a person who "falls." What else might this imply besides physically falling down?

A good friend is supportive of you and in times of sadness and upset, we can lean on our friends for emotional support. We also serve as a support system for our friends when they need it and celebrate each others' achievements.

- *Do you feel the pain of a friend who is suffering?*
- *How would you help a friend who is in trouble?*

Think of a metaphor for the support of a good friend. Explain your metaphor
"A supportive friend is like a _____ *"*

Do you need to be friends with everyone?

It is unrealistic to think that every person will like you, and that you will like every person. You don't have to be best friends with everyone. You undoubtedly know people with whom you do not want to be friends, or that you would be smart to stay away from. For example, if you know someone who engages in illegal or risky behavior, you should think twice before being friends with that person. However, this does not mean that person needs to be your enemy, or someone whom you treat with disrespect; just someone with whom you do not associate.

Judaism recognizes the important role people around you play in shaping your values, attitudes and actions. The recognition of that reality underlies the following texts:

נִתַּאי הָאַרְבֵּלִי אוֹמֵר, הַרְחֵק מִשָּׁכֵן רָע, וְאַל תִּתְחַבֵּר לָרָשָׁע, וְאַל תִּתְיָאֵשׁ מִן הַפֻּרְעָנוּת :

Nattai the Arbelite, said "Keep yourself far from a bad neighbor, don't associate with the wicked, and don't abandon the belief in retribution."

(Pirkei Avot 1:7)

"Never be weary of making friends; consider a single enemy as one too many. If you have a faithful friend, hold fast to him. Let him not go, for he is a precious possession. "

(Asher b. Yehiel, 13th century Germany and Spain)

- **These two texts seem to be conflicting—how do we resolve the apparent contradiction?**
- **The first second tells us that we should always be striving to make friends. Do you agree?**

Take a look at the following Tefillah, recited early in the Shacharit service:

יְהִי רָצוֹן מִלְּפָנֶיךָ, יְיָ אֱלֹהַי וֵאלֹהֵי אֲבוֹתַי, שֶׁתַּצִּילֵנִי הַיּוֹם וּבְכָל יוֹם מֵעַזֵּי פָנִים וּמֵעַזּוּת פָּנִים, מֵאָדָם רָע, וּמֵחָבֵר רָע, וּמִשָּׁכֵן רָע, וּמִפֶּגַע רָע, וּמִשָּׂטָן הַמַּשְׁחִית, מִדִּין קָשֶׁה, וּמִבַּעַל דִּין קָשֶׁה, בֵּין שֶׁהוּא בֶן בְּרִית, וּבֵין שֶׁאֵינוֹ בֶן בְּרִית.

May it be Your will, Lord my God and God of my ancestors, to protect me this day and everyday from insolence in others and arrogance in myself. Save me from vicious people, from evil neighbors and from corrupt companions. Preserve me from misfortune and from powers of destruction. Save me from harsh judgments, spare me from ruthless opponents, be they members of the covenant or not.

(Shacharit service, Sim Shalom, p13)

Activity: In Your Own Words

Try to reword the prayer from the Shacharit service asking God that you be saved from the influence of evil companions and neighbors. Put it in your own language.

The Brit of Friendship

What is a *brit*? In Bereishit, we read twice a *brit,* commonly translated as a "covenant" or "contract," as an agreement between a person and God. In Noah's case, (Bereishit 9:15) he and God have an agreement that God will never again bring flood waters to the world to destroy everything. In Abraham's case (Bereishit 15:18) he and God have an agreement that the land of Canaan will be for Abraham's descendants to inherit.

How is friendship a kind of brit? Similar to a covenant or contract, there are "terms" under which two people remain friends, and a sense of loyalty and faithfulness ensuring that the brit is maintained.

The friendship of David and Jonathan as portrayed in the biblical book of Shmuel is held in great esteem. In this friendship, both David and Jonathan give totally of themselves to each other, but do not make demands upon the other. In the First Book of Shmuel (20:18-42) [the Haftarah of Machar Chodesh, read on the Sabbath of the eve of Rosh Chodesh], the friendship of Jonathan and David is further amplified. After David's victory against the powerful Goliath, King Saul, who is Jonathan's father, has become suspicious of David. But Jonathan remains completely loyal to David, who goes into hiding after realizing that his life is in danger. The biblical passage concludes with a description of a prearranged code by which Jonathan informs his best friend David to flee for his life. The story clearly shows the deep loyalty of these best friends for each other. We will look further at the relationship between David and Jonathan shortly.

Jonathan and David have a pact— a brit— of friendship and loyalty. We will return to the narrative about David and Jonathan later in the chapter. The following mishnah from Pirkei Avot refers to their friendship:

כָּל אַהֲבָה שֶׁהִיא תְלוּיָה בְדָבָר, בָּטֵל דָּבָר, בְּטֵלָה אַהֲבָה. וְשֶׁאֵינָה תְּלוּיָה בְדָבָר, אֵינָה בְּטֵלָה לְעוֹלָם. אֵיזוֹ הִיא אַהֲבָה הַתְּלוּיָה בְדָבָר, זוֹ אַהֲבַת אַמְנוֹן וְתָמָר. וְשֶׁאֵינָה תְּלוּיָה בְדָבָר, זוֹ אַהֲבַת דָּוִד וִיהוֹנָתָן:	All love which depends on some material cause and the material cause passes away, the love passes away too. But if it is not dependent on some material cause, it will never pass away. Which love was depended on some material cause? The love of Amnon and Tamar. And which depended on nothing selfish? The love of David and Jonathan.

(Pirkei Avot 5: 19)

(Note: Tamar was the daughter of David and sister of Absalom. She was raped by her stepbrother Amnon (II Shmuel 13) who was slain for his action by Absalom.)

When you make a friend, begin by testing him, and be in no hurry to trust him.
Some friends are loyal when it suits them, but desert you in time of trouble.
Some friends turn into enemies and shame you by making the quarrel public.
Another sits at your table but is nowhere to be found in time of trouble.
When you are prosperous, he will be your second self and make free with your servants, but if you come down in the world, he will turn against you and you will not see him again.
Hold your enemies at a distance, and keep a wary eye on your friends.
A faithful friend is a secure shelter; whoever finds one has found a treasure.

A faithful friend is beyond price; his worth is more than money can buy ...
Do not desert an old friend. A new one is not worth as much.
A new friend is like new wine. You do not enjoy drinking it until is has matured.

(Wisdom of Ben Sira, 6:7-15, 9:10)

Here is a story adapted from Pirkei de Rabbi Eliezer, an eighth century midrashic work:

A person had three friends. One friend he loved very much, the second he loved as well. The third friend was regarded with less affection. Once the king commanded this person to appear before him. The person was extremely agitated, wondering what the king might have in mind. With fear and trepidation, the person called upon each of his three friends to accompany him at his meeting with the king. First, he turned to his most beloved friend, and was extremely disappointed that this friend was unable to attend his meeting with the king.

Turning to his second friend, the friend replied that indeed he would go with him, but only so far as the gates of the palace, but no further. Finally, and with a touch of desperation, he turned to his friend to whom he had been the least devoted.

This friend said: "I will not only go with you before the king, but I will plead your case as well"

Who was the first friend? It is a person's wealth and material things which he must leave behind when he departs this world, as it is written: "Riches profit not in the day of reckoning. " Who was the second friend? It is a person's relatives, who can only follow him to the graveside, as it is written: "No person can by any means redeem his fellow human being from death. " The third friend, the least considered one, is the good deeds of a person's life. These never leave him and even precede him to plead his cause before the King of Kings, as it is written: "And your righteousness shall go before you."

What is the moral of the Pirkei de Rabbi Eliezar story of the three friends? Do you agree with the moral of the story?

How do you personally go about making friends? Did your friendships simply occur by accident, or were they a conscious effort on your or your friends' part?

For Further Thought

1. Think of a time when your friends convinced you to do something you didn't think was right. How did it happen? Why did you let it happen? How might it have been avoided?

2. Think of a time when you convinced someone else to do something that he/she did not want to do. Why did you do it? Were you aware of the other person's resistance? Was the resistance a challenge for you to overcome or was your own desire more important? How might your friends have convinced you to stop your encouragement?

3. Think of a time when your friends encouraged you to do something that you didn't want to do, but which you knew you should do. How did you feel about them? Did it affect your friendship in any way, positively or negatively? Was it easier to overcome your reluctance because of the support you received from your friends?

4. *Did you ever encourage you friends to do something that you were convinced they should do or was in their best interest, even though they were reluctant to do so? How did you feel afterwards? Did it affect your friendship with them?*

5. *Has your friend ever let you down or disappointed you? How did you handle this? What did it teach you about the friendship? What did it teach you about the person?*

Activity: The Brit Bracelets

David and Jonathan make a pact with each other to protect each other and remain loyal. God makes a promise to Noah never to cause such a flood again and gives the rainbow as a sign of that promise.

Imagine you and your best friend create a *brit* or contract together. What would it look like? What "deal" would you make between the two of you (and God!) that would illustrate loyalty? How does a brit define the idea of loyalty?

What words do you think are important to include in your brit?

רַבִּי אֱלִיעֶזֶר אוֹמֵר, יְהִי כְּבוֹד חֲבֵרְךָ חָבִיב עָלֶיךָ כְּשֶׁלָּךְ Let the honor of your friend be as dear to you as your own.

(Pirkei Avot 2:15)

The following is a story that illustrates the brit of friendship:

At the time of the Roman Empire, two Jewish boys had grown up together in Israel and become very close friends. After awhile, they moved far apart - one living under Roman control, and the other living under Syrian control. Yet they remained very close friends.

One time, when the fellow from Rome was visiting in Syria, someone falsely accused him of being a spy. They brought him to the Syrian Emperor, and he was sentenced to death. As he was being led out to be executed, they asked if he had any last requests. "Please, let me go back to Rome to settle my affairs and say goodbye to my family. Then I'll come back and you can execute me."

The Emperor laughed. "Are you crazy? What guarantee do I have that you'll come back?" The Jew said, "I have a friend here in Syria who will stand in for me. He'll be my guarantor. If I don't come back, you can kill him instead." The Emperor was intrigued, and the Syrian Jew was called in. Sure enough, he agreed to take his friend's place in prison, and be killed instead if the friend did not return. The Emperor was so startled by this arrangement that he agreed to let the Roman Jew go. "I will give you 60 days. If you're not back by the dawn of the 60th day, your friend dies."

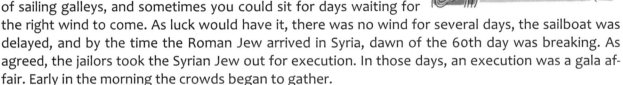

The Roman Jew raced back to say goodbye and put his affairs in order. After a hectic time and a lot of tears, he started back in plenty of time before the 60 days were up. But those were the days of sailing galleys, and sometimes you could sit for days waiting for the right wind to come. As luck would have it, there was no wind for several days, the sailboat was delayed, and by the time the Roman Jew arrived in Syria, dawn of the 60th day was breaking. As agreed, the jailors took the Syrian Jew out for execution. In those days, an execution was a gala affair. Early in the morning the crowds began to gather.

Finally, as they were just about to perform the execution, the Roman Jew came running in. "Wait! I'm back. Don't kill him!" But the Syrian Jew protested: "You can't kill him. He came too late. I'm the guarantor. You've got to kill me instead!" Each friend was equally adamant. "Kill me!" "No, kill me instead!" The executioner didn't know what to do. The crowd was in an uproar! Finally, the Emperor was called. In wonder and amazement, he turned to the two of them and said, "I'll let both of you go free on one condition. That you make me your third friend!"

- *Why is the Emperor impressed by this friendship?*
- *How do you exhibit loyalty toward a friend?*
- *Think about the friendships you've had that have dissolved. How does loyalty contribute to maintaining a friendship?*
- *This friend was willing to give up his own life to save his friend. Although this is a very extreme example, should friendship require some sort of sacrifice as a sign of loyalty?*

Earlier we discussed the concept of the *brit* of friendship. But now let's think about how far that *brit* extends. While there must be a level of trust between friends, if a friend is self-harming, or discussing harming him or herself, your *brit* is overridden by this behavior and any implied or explicit promises you have with your friend about keeping that behavior confidential may be broken. Your responsibility as a friend is to save your friend's life by seeking out help from an adult. Similarly, we must be careful not to enable a friend's wrongful behavior if it puts him or her in danger or is illegal activity.

Brit or loyalty is a key characteristic of friendship. What about negative friendships or friendships that could be draining on you- should you be loyal to these friends?

Can you think of a situation where you would not want to support a friend? For example, would there be a time when your support would be enabling bad behavior? Do you always have to be there for a friend? What types of situations would you choose not to support?

Let's look at a part of the story of Noah. In Bereishit 9:19- 23 we read:

יט שְׁלֹשָׁה אֵלֶּה, בְּנֵי-נֹחַ; וּמֵאֵלֶּה, נָפְצָה כָל-הָאָרֶץ.	**19** These three were the sons of Noah, and of these was the whole earth overspread.
כ וַיָּחֶל נֹחַ, אִישׁ הָאֲדָמָה; וַיִּטַּע, כָּרֶם.	**20** And Noah the husbandman began, and planted a vineyard.
כא וַיֵּשְׁתְּ מִן-הַיַּיִן, וַיִּשְׁכָּר; וַיִּתְגַּל, בְּתוֹךְ אָהֳלֹה.	**21** And he drank of the wine, and was drunken; and he was uncovered within his tent.
כב וַיַּרְא, חָם אֲבִי כְנַעַן, אֵת, עֶרְוַת אָבִיו; וַיַּגֵּד לִשְׁנֵי-אֶחָיו, בַּחוּץ.	**22** And Ham, the father of Canaan, saw the nakedness of his father, and told his two brethren without.
כג וַיִּקַּח שֵׁם וָיֶפֶת אֶת-הַשִּׂמְלָה, וַיָּשִׂימוּ עַל-שְׁכֶם שְׁנֵיהֶם, וַיֵּלְכוּ אֲחֹרַנִּית, וַיְכַסּוּ אֵת עֶרְוַת אֲבִיהֶם; וּפְנֵיהֶם, אֲחֹרַנִּית, וְעֶרְוַת אֲבִיהֶם, לֹא רָאוּ.	**23** And Shem and Japheth took a garment, and laid it upon both their shoulders, and went backward, and covered the nakedness of their father; and their faces were backward, and they saw not their father's nakedness.

Let's look at what happens in this story: Noah has a drink of wine. It's possible that he didn't intend to get drunk but he did. That might sound familiar – maybe you're at a party, and there's alcohol. You have a drink. You get drunk. It may have been unintended but it happened as a natural result of your action. Did Noah get undressed because he was drunk? That might happen at a party also. Perhaps you've drank too much and you start acting inappropriately— in a way that you wouldn't act otherwise. What might the other party goers do? One of your 'friends' sees you, tells everyone to come look, i.e. to take advantage of you in your drunken state. Your real friends refuse, they take care of you instead. They realize you are vulnerable, exposed, not in charge of your senses and they don't let it go further. These are true friends, friends worth having, the kind of friend you want to be.

אַל תָּדִין אֶת חֲבֵרְךָ עַד שֶׁתַּגִּיעַ לִמְקוֹמוֹ Do not judge your friend until you put yourself in his position.

(Pirkei Avot 2:5)

Activity: Consider these scenarios:

Scenario 1:

A week after Greg turned eighteen, Zach, his sixteen-year-old friend, asks to borrow his ID to buy cigarettes. Greg has never supported his friend's bad habit, and quickly reasons that they look nothing alike, so Greg's ID wouldn't work anyway. Zach tells him that they have the same hair color, and no one actually looks that closely, so it would be fine. Greg knows Zach would buy cigarettes even if he didn't help him out, but is still concerned that if Zach is caught using a fake ID, it could be taken away, and Greg would end up either without a license or in trouble for helping a minor to buy tobacco.

- What should Greg do? What if you knew that neither of you would get caught or in trouble?
- How would your answer differ if Zach wanted to borrow an ID to buy something else (alcohol, pornography, etc.)? Why?
- What are the possible consequences of enabling Zach in this scenario?
- Do you think that refusing to help Zach in this one circumstance would help the greater problem of Zach's (underage) smoking?
- With whom does Greg have a Brit in this situation? With himself or his friend?

Scenario 2:

Susan met Jake on Facebook®. Rachel has never been comfortable with her best friend talking to someone she doesn't actually know, even though they have many mutual friends and she has only heard good things about him, but figures that it's not a big deal if their contact remains only online. But one day, Susan tells Rachel that she is planning on meeting Jake in person, and wants to know if Rachel will drive her to her date. Susan knows her parents would not approve, and worries what their other friends might think about seeing him in person, so she tells Rachel not to tell anyone. Susan says they're planning to meet up in a public setting and that she will be sure to have her cell phone on her, just for good measure. But Rachel is still uneasy about the whole situation.

- What are the potential dangers of this situation for Susan? For Rachel?
- What would you do if you were Rachel? Would you tell someone else? Would you help Susan get to her date?
- What Jewish value that you know of did Susan need to employ to ensure her safety (hint: watching your words isn't just what you say but what you type!)?
- Would you doubt Rachel's loyalty if you were Susan and she refused to drive you
- As an outsider, would you doubt Rachel's loyalty if she were to drive Susan or not drive Susan?
- Do you think teens should be discouraged from meeting online friends in person? Why?

Biblical Bonds of Friendship

Let's look at a few examples of friendship from the *Tanach*. In each case, the bonds of friendship were tested by outside forces, and the bond held strong. Let's examine the previously mentioned narrative of David and Jonathan a little closer:

David and Jonathan

David is a warrior who impresses King Saul. He becomes good friends, loyal like a brother with Jonathan, King Saul's son.

יז וַיּוֹסֶף יְהוֹנָתָן לְהַשְׁבִּיעַ אֶת־דָּוִד, בְּאַהֲבָתוֹ אֹתוֹ : כִּי־אַהֲבַת נַפְשׁוֹ, אֲהֵבוֹ.

17 And Jonathan caused David to swear again, for the love that he had to him; for he loved him as he loved his own soul.

יח וַיֹּאמֶר־לוֹ יְהוֹנָתָן, מָחָר חֹדֶשׁ ; וְנִפְקַדְתָּ, כִּי יִפָּקֵד מוֹשָׁבֶךָ.

18 And Jonathan said unto him: 'Tomorrow is the new moon; and you will be missed, your seat will be empty.

(I Shmuel 18:17-18)

But eventually, Saul becomes jealous of David's victories in war and wants to kill him; he calls his son Jonathan into his chambers and tells him to kill David. Although Jonathan knows his father could punish him, even kill him, Jonathan risks his life and reveals the plot to David:

וַיַּגֵּד יְהוֹנָתָן לְדָוִד לֵאמֹר מְבַקֵּשׁ שָׁאוּל אָבִי לַהֲמִיתֶךָ וְעַתָּה הִשָּׁמֶר נָא בַבֹּקֶר וְיָשַׁבְתָּ בַסֵּתֶר וְנַחְבֵּאתָ : ג וַאֲנִי אֵצֵא וְעָמַדְתִּי לְיַד אָבִי בַּשָּׂדֶה אֲשֶׁר אַתָּה שָׁם וַאֲנִי אֲדַבֵּר בְּךָ אֶל־אָבִי וְרָאִיתִי מָה וְהִגַּדְתִּי לָךְ :

'My father Saul is bent on killing you. Be on your guard tomorrow morning; get to a secret place and remain in hiding. I will go out and stand next to my father in the field where you will be, and I will speak to my father about you. If I learn anything, I will tell you.'

(I Shmuel 19:2-3)

Jonathan pleads David's case to his father, and Saul agrees not to kill him. But David continues to be victorious in battle after battle, and an evil spirit overtakes Saul, who again seeks to kill David. When Jonathan again pleads his case, Saul flies into a rage and yells at Jonathan:

ל וַיִּחַר־אַף שָׁאוּל בִּיהוֹנָתָן וַיֹּאמֶר לוֹ בֶּן־נַעֲוַת הַמַּרְדּוּת הֲלוֹא יָדַעְתִּי כִּי־בֹחֵר אַתָּה לְבֶן־יִשַׁי לְבָשְׁתְּךָ וּלְבֹשֶׁת עֶרְוַת אִמֶּךָ : לֹא כִּי כָל־הַיָּמִים אֲשֶׁר בֶּן־יִשַׁי חַי עַל־הָאֲדָמָה לֹא תִכּוֹן אַתָּה וּמַלְכוּתֶךָ וְעַתָּה שְׁלַח וְקַח אֹתוֹ אֵלַי כִּי בֶן־מָוֶת הוּא

30 You son of a perverse, rebellious woman! I know that you side with the son of Jesse [David]—to your shame! For as long as the son of Jesse lives on earth, neither you nor your kingship will be secure. Now then, have him brought to me, for he is marked for death.

(I Shmuel 20:30)

But this does not stop Jonathan from helping his friend. Throughout the following years, as Saul tries many times to find a way to kill David, Jonathan helps save him. They do not see each other for many years, but their friendship remains strong. But in a battle against Amalek, Saul and Jonathan are killed.

וַיַּחֲזֵק דָּוִד בִּבְגָדָו [בִּבְגָדָיו] וַיִּקְרָעֵם וְגַם כָּל־הָאֲנָשִׁים אֲשֶׁר אִתּוֹ : וַיִּסְפְּדוּ וַיִּבְכּוּ וַיָּצֻמוּ עַד־הָעֶרֶב עַל־שָׁאוּל וְעַל־יְהוֹנָתָן בְּנוֹ וְעַל־עַם יְהוָה וְעַל־בֵּית יִשְׂרָאֵל כִּי נָפְלוּ בֶּחָרֶב
וַיְקֹנֵן דָּוִד אֶת־הַקִּינָה הַזֹּאת עַל־שָׁאוּל וְעַל־יְהוֹנָתָן בְּנוֹ

David took hold of his clothes and rent them, and so did all the men with him. They lamented and wept, and they fasted until evening for Saul and his son Jonathan... And David lamented with this lamentation over Saul and over Jonathan his son;"

(II Shmuel 1:11-12, 17)

- *What characterizes David and Jonathan's relationship?*
- *What specific words are used in the exchange between them?*
- *How is their friendship tested?*
- *Does their friendship prevail? Why?*
- *When David hears that Saul and Jonathan have been slain, he mourns for both—what does this say about his character, that he can mourn for someone who sought to kill him?*
- *Think back to the text "consider a single enemy as one too many."*
- *How did David exemplify this? How do you think he was able to do that?*

David had every right to dislike Saul, who was the true definition of David's enemy. David did nothing to provoke Saul's hatred, yet Saul sought to kill him for years. But David still mourned him when he died; he did not reciprocate Saul's hatred.

Ruth and Naomi

Now let's look at the famous story of Naomi and Ruth from Megillat Ruth that we read on the holiday of Shavuot. Naomi's two sons die shortly after her husband's death, leaving her alone. She returns from Moab to Judah with her daughters in law, Ruth and Orpah:

א וַיְהִי, בִּימֵי שְׁפֹט הַשֹּׁפְטִים, וַיְהִי רָעָב, בָּאָרֶץ; וַיֵּלֶךְ אִישׁ מִבֵּית לֶחֶם יְהוּדָה, לָגוּר בִּשְׂדֵי מוֹאָב--הוּא וְאִשְׁתּוֹ, וּשְׁנֵי בָנָיו.

1 And it came to pass in the days when the judges judged, that there was a famine in the land. And a certain man of Beth-lehem in Judah went to sojourn in the field of Moab, he, and his wife, and his two sons.

ב וְשֵׁם הָאִישׁ אֱלִימֶלֶךְ וְשֵׁם אִשְׁתּוֹ נָעֳמִי וְשֵׁם שְׁנֵי־בָנָיו מַחְלוֹן וְכִלְיוֹן, אֶפְרָתִים--מִבֵּית לֶחֶם, יְהוּדָה; וַיָּבֹאוּ שְׂדֵי־מוֹאָב, וַיִּהְיוּ־שָׁם.

2 And the name of the man was Elimelech, and the name of his wife Naomi, and the name of his two sons Mahlon and Chilion, Ephrathites of Beth-lehem in Judah. And they came into the field of Moab, and continued there.

ג וַיָּמָת אֱלִימֶלֶךְ, אִישׁ נָעֳמִי; וַתִּשָּׁאֵר הִיא, וּשְׁנֵי בָנֶיהָ.

3 And Elimelech Naomi's husband died; and she was left, and her two sons.

ד וַיִּשְׂאוּ לָהֶם, נָשִׁים מֹאֲבִיּוֹת--שֵׁם הָאַחַת עָרְפָּה, וְשֵׁם הַשֵּׁנִית רוּת; וַיֵּשְׁבוּ שָׁם, כְּעֶשֶׂר שָׁנִים.

4 And they took them wives of the women of Moab: the name of the one was Orpah, and the name of the other Ruth; and they dwelt there about ten years.

ה וַיָּמֻתוּ גַם־שְׁנֵיהֶם, מַחְלוֹן וְכִלְיוֹן; וַתִּשָּׁאֵר, הָאִשָּׁה, מִשְּׁנֵי יְלָדֶיהָ, וּמֵאִישָׁהּ.

5 And Mahlon and Chilion died both of them; and the woman was left of her two children and of her husband.

וֹ וַתָּקָם הִיא וְכַלֹּתֶיהָ, וַתָּשָׁב מִשְּׂדֵי מוֹאָב: כִּי שָׁמְעָה, בִּשְׂדֵה מוֹאָב--כִּי-פָקַד יְהוָה אֶת-עַמּוֹ, לָתֵת לָהֶם לָחֶם.

6 Then she rose with her daughters-in-law, that she might return from the field of Moab; for she had heard in the field of Moab how that God had remembered God's people in giving them bread.

ז וַתֵּצֵא, מִן-הַמָּקוֹם אֲשֶׁר הָיְתָה-שָׁמָּה, וּשְׁתֵּי כַלֹּתֶיהָ, עִמָּהּ; וַתֵּלַכְנָה בַדֶּרֶךְ, לָשׁוּב אֶל-אֶרֶץ יְהוּדָה.

7 And she went forth out of the place where she was, and her two daughters-in-law with her; and they went on the way to return unto the land of Judah.

Naomi encourages her daughters in law to return to their families but they insist to remain by her side. Finally, Orpah kisses her goodbye while Ruth stays with her mother-in-law.

ח וַתֹּאמֶר נָעֳמִי, לִשְׁתֵּי כַלֹּתֶיהָ, לֵכְנָה שֹּׁבְנָה, אִשָּׁה לְבֵית אִמָּהּ; יעשה (יַעַשׂ) יְהוָה עִמָּכֶם חֶסֶד, כַּאֲשֶׁר עֲשִׂיתֶם עִם-הַמֵּתִים וְעִמָּדִי.

8 And Naomi said unto her two daughters-in-law: 'Go, return each of you to her mother's house; the Lord deal kindly with you, as you have dealt with the dead, and with me.

ט יִתֵּן יְהוָה, לָכֶם, וּמְצֶאןָ מְנוּחָה, אִשָּׁה בֵּית אִישָׁהּ; וַתִּשַּׁק לָהֶן, וַתִּשֶּׂאנָה קוֹלָן וַתִּבְכֶּינָה.

9 The Lord grant you that you may find rest, each of you in the house of her husband.' Then she kissed them; and they lifted up their voice, and wept.

י וַתֹּאמַרְנָה-לָּהּ: כִּי-אִתָּךְ נָשׁוּב, לְעַמֵּךְ.

10 And they said unto her: 'No, but we will return with you to your people.'

And she [Naomi] said: "Your sister in law has returned to her people...Return with your sister in law." And Ruth said: "Do not ask me to leave you, or to return from following after you; for wherever you go, I will go... where you die, will I die, and there will I be buried..." When Naomi saw that Ruth was steadfastly minded to go with her, then she [Naomi] stopped speaking.

(Megillat Ruth 1:8-17)

- *What characterizes Naomi and Ruth's relationship?*
- *Orpah leaves Naomi but Ruth remains with her, telling her that Naomi's people will be her people and Naomi's God will be her God. What does this say about Ruth?*
- *Is this friendship or familial obligation [note that Naomi and the other two women were related through marriage, not blood]*
- *How is their friendship tested? How does Ruth show her loyalty?*
- *Does their friendship prevail? Why?*
- *Why does Orpah leave but Ruth stays? Do you think one of them made a better choice?*
- *According to these two stories, how would you explain the Jewish view on friendship?*
- *How is loyalty a Jewish characteristic? Where else do we see loyalty as a Judaic or Jewish trait (i.e. God's loyalty)?*

Ruth was willing to do anything to remain by Naomi's side. How do you determine your own loyalty toward a friend? Does it depend on the degree of your friendship?

What would you give up for a friend?

Should friendship require sacrifice of some kind? Is sacrifice a sign of loyalty? What are some signs of loyalty?

Try completing this sentence:
Loyalty is _____.

Activity: The Loyalty Line
Where does your loyalty lie?

Draw the line at where your loyalty to a friend would end. How do you determine what you'd do for a friend? What would the friends in your life do for you? Look at the items below. Then, plot each one onto the line using the letters:

⟵――――――――――――――――――――――――――――――――――――――⟶

NOPE, NOT EVEN FOR A FRIEND   ABSOLUTELY

a. I'd lend something to a friend
b. I'd attend a friend's special event even if I don't want to
c. I'd stand up to a bully for a friend
d. I'd change my plans for a friend
e. I'd travel to a different country for a friend
f. I'd give up something special (material or not) for a friend
g. I'd lie for a friend
h. I'd hurt someone else for a friend
i. I'd disappoint my family members for a friend
j. I'd make uncharacteristic decisions (things I wouldn't normally do) for a friend
k. I'd put myself in danger for a friend

Activity: Taking Stock
The types or degrees of friendship
Consider the levels of friendship. Can you relate David and Jonathan's friendship or Ruth and Naomi's to a relationship you have? What degrees of friendship do you have in your life?

Who would you consider:

Your "fun friend"—someone you call upon to do something fun. _____

Your loyal friend—someone you know will always be there. _____

Your on-and-off friend—your friendship depends on specific factors. _____

Your "forever friend"—someone you've been friends with since you were babies/ preschool _____

Your "family friend"— someone who is your friend through familial association. _____

Your lifelong best friend. _____

The "Oys" of Friendship

17 You shall not hate your brother in your heart; יי לֹא-תִשְׂנָא אֶת-אָחִיךָ, בִּלְבָבֶךָ.

(Vayikra 19:17)

You know that "hate" is a powerful word, but sometimes our friends disappoint us, resulting in conflict. What are arguments between friends often about?

Rephrase this quote from Mishlei into your own words. At what point do you stop forgiving your friends for hurting you? Does forgiveness cure all friendship woes?

9 One who covers a transgression seeks love; but one that that repeats a matter separates him/herself from a familiar friend. ט מְכַסֶּה-פֶּשַׁע, מְבַקֵּשׁ אַהֲבָה; וְשֹׁנֶה בְדָבָר, מַפְרִיד אַלּוּף.

(Mishlei 17:9)

Your friends will anger, disappoint or frustrate you more than once, but Tshuvah and forgiveness is the answer to making sure the friendship doesn't end each time a friend disappoints you. Tshuvah—to change our ways, to "turn back" and say "slichah"— I'm sorry. On the other hand, is there ever anything a friend can do that is unforgivable? Does regret, remorse and Tshuvah magically solve all problems between friends? How sincere is the regret? How authentic is the Tshuvah?

Activity: Her Story, His Story, My Story

Conflict is all about perspective. In the space below, describe a recent argument you've had with a friend. What triggered it? Was it an action? Something that was said? Were harsh words exchanged or feelings hurt?

In the second space provided, try expressing the same story first from your perspective and then from the other person's perspective. Sometimes, a lack of empathy can cause argument.

My Story:

His/Her Story:

Tshuvah between friends

The Rambam tells us there are four steps to Tshuvah: (1) ceasing to do what caused the other person pain in the first place (2) admitting to your errors verbally- to yourself and to the other person (3) expressing shame and regret for having hurt the person (4) the taking upon oneself never to do, act or think that way again. (paraphrased from Hilchot Tshuvah chapters 1, 2)

- *What would you add or change to these four steps?*
- *Do you think these steps are natural as a way of expressing regret and asking for forgiveness? Is this common sense?*
- *How does this process make both parties feel respected and ease the tension?*
- *Why is each step important to repairing a strained relationship with a friend?*
- *Why is Tshuvah so difficult to do? Why do we hold grudges?*
- *What is your own personal order of Tshuvah? What are the steps it takes to make up with a friend?*

Rabbi Beroka of Khuzistan often visited the market at Lapat. There he would meet Elijah the Prophet.

"Does anyone in this market have a share in the World to Come?" Rabbi Beroka asked one day.

While they were talking, two men came by. Elijah said, "Those two have a share in the World to Come." Rabbi Beroka went to them and said, "What do you do?"

They said, "We are jesters. When we see a person depressed, we try to cheer him up. And when we see two friends that are quarreling, we work hard to make peace between them." (Ta'anit 22a)

Who is a leader? Any person can turn an enemy into one's friend. (Avot d'Rabbi Natan, Chapter 23)

Friendship is complicated. **But what happens when you take friendship to the next level?**

Part Two

בֵּין אָדָם לְעַצְמוֹ
Bein Adam L'Atzmo
me, myself and I

Before we can continue to explore our relationships with others, we need to take a closer look at ourselves.

In this section, we will explore our interpersonal relationships through a look at individuality and equality, discover how we are created *B'tzelem Elohim* (in the image of God), see how our dress and words affect our relationships, and finally, explore what it means to be a "*mensch.*"

Chapter Three
Individuality and Equality

You may feel pressure to be in a relationship, but should feel that you are a complete person whether or not you have a romantic partner. Even when we are in relationships, it is critical to maintain our individuality, despite stereotypes which often serve to diminish our ability to express our individuality. Gender differences are never a reason for gender barriers and each person in a relationship should be valued equally.

וַיִּבְרָא אֱלֹהִים | אֶת־הָאָדָם בְּצַלְמוֹ בְּצֶלֶם אֱלֹהִים בָּרָא אֹתוֹ זָכָר וּנְקֵבָה בָּרָא אֹתָם

And God created Adam in God's image, in the image of God, God created **him**, male and female God created **them**.

(Bereishit 1:27)

Rashi explains: Later it says 'And He took one of his sides...' Midrash Aggadah [resolves the apparent contradiction by explaining] that he was created with two faces in the first creation, and afterwards separated.'

What contradiction is Rashi explaining here?

The text says that God created "him," a singular pronoun, but at the end of the phrase it says God created "them," a plural pronoun. According to the Midrash, God first created a single entity that was both male and female, and then afterward split the creature into two <u>equal</u> and <u>individual</u> entities.

Activity: What makes a complete person?

What character traits make a complete person? Are there certain ones that you would attribute to both male and female? The traits are individual pieces that come together to form one whole.

Write the traits that you believe to be "female" in the woman's puzzle piece and those you believe to be "male" in the man's.

What can we learn about relationships from the way in which God created Adam and Eve?

יח נַיֹּאמֶר יְהוָה אֱלֹהִים, לֹא-טוֹב הֱיוֹת הָאָדָם לְבַדּוֹ; אֶעֱשֶׂה-לּוֹ עֵזֶר, כְּנֶגְדּוֹ.

18 It is not good for man to be alone; I will make a fitting helper for him.

(Bereishit 2:18)

When they were first created, Adam and Eve were connected—literally. But God realized something: If you look at the text, you can interpret God's statement, לֹא-טוֹב הֱיוֹת הָאָדָם לְבַדּוֹ as "It is not good for humans to be singular." Every person is unique and is an individual. Even when we are connected to each other in a dating relationship, it is very important to maintain our own individuality.

Activity: Will the real me please stand up?

What makes me unique?

I am good at_____

A childhood nickname for me was _____

My secret hidden talent is _____

A pet peeve of mine is _____

My favorite thing to do on weekends is _____

Something that scares me is _____

Add your own- what makes you unique? What about yourself would you like to share with someone else?

Compare your answers with those of a friend. What distinguishes you from each other? What commonalities do you have? Among all of your relationships, you will have commonalities and differences that distinguish you from your neighbor. Among the different relationships in your life, each partner or half will bring his/her individuality to the pair. Whatever you interaction may be—with a parent, teacher or best friend, be who you want, but always be you!

Sometimes, you might feel pressure to be in a relationship and have a boyfriend or girlfriend. While it can be a lot of fun to be in a relationship, being in a dating relationship should not change what you think or how you act. Being in a relationship should never define who you are. You are still you! **And if you're not in a relationship, that's fine too.** You can be you without being attached to someone. Although sometimes it may seem as if everyone either is or wants to be in a relationship, take a good look around – many happy people are not in relationships and are leading full and interesting lives.

Remember, God split Adam and Eve into two because one person is a whole person all by his or herself.

Do you feel pressure to be in a relationship? Even if you don't feel it, do you think there generally there is pressure to be in one? If yes, where does that pressure come from? Is it from your friends? Your parents? TV shows or movies?
What if you don't want to be in a relationship? Is that okay or do you feel insecure about that decision? How do you deal with any of these pressures?

כא וַיַּפֵּל יְהֹוָה אֱלֹהִים תַּרְדֵּמָה עַל־הָאָדָם, וַיִּישָׁן; וַיִּקַּח, אַחַת מִצַּלְעֹתָיו, וַיִּסְגֹּר בָּשָׂר, תַּחְתֶּנָּה.

21 And the Lord God caused a deep sleep to fall upon the man, and he slept; and God took one of his ribs, and closed up the place with flesh instead thereof.

כב וַיִּבֶן יְהֹוָה אֱלֹהִים אֶת־הַצֵּלָע אֲשֶׁר־לָקַח מִן־הָאָדָם, לְאִשָּׁה; וַיְבִאֶהָ, אֶל־הָאָדָם.

22 And the rib, which the Lord God had taken from the man, God made a woman, and brought her unto the man.

(Bereishit 2:21-22)

The text above says that Eve was created, אַחַת מִצַּלְעֹתָיו commonly translated as "from one of Adam's ribs." However, if we accept the idea that Adam and Eve were originally one creature, and then later were separated, we can interpret this as Eve being created "from one of Adam's sides," or half of Adam. Does this change the meaning?

This translation emphasizes a sense of equality, which is critical in a relationship. Eve was not simply created from a part of Adam; they were created from equal parts of the same being. They maintain a connection, if not physical anymore, but are still unique and individual.

טז דּוֹדִי לִי וַאֲנִי לוֹ, הָרֹעֶה בַּשּׁוֹשַׁנִּים.   **16** I am my beloved's, and my beloved is mine.

(Shir HaShirim 2:16)

What can we learn from this verse about equality in relationships?

Good relationships are based on cooperation and teamwork as well as giving and receiving. Let's do an activity to illustrate how working together can help us achieve our goals.

In order to give to and take from another, you need to be sure of who you are as an individual.

Activity: Cooperation in Relationships

Find a partner. Sit back to back on the floor and loop your arms together so you are "connected." First, have your friend try to stand up by his or her self. Then try to stand up by yourself. Last, try and stand up working together.

What happened when only one person tried to get up? Why?
Why were you able to get up together? Was this easy to do?
How does working in partnership make for a healthy relationship?

Think about who you are and what you need from others and what you are willing to give.

Activity: A Recipe for Individuality

Just like God created Adam and Eve, he created you. What recipe do you think He used? If you were to write a recipe for creating yourself, what would it contain? Feel free to use the template below, and add anything you like—and be creative!

Recipe Serves: ONE

Dish: Recipe for ME

Ingredients:

Directions:
A cup of _____
_____
_____

A pinch of _____
A handful of _____
A splash of _____
A hint of _____

Individuality v. Conformity

שאדם טובע כמה מטבעות בחותם אחד - כולן דומין זה לזה, ומלך מלכי המלכים הקדוש ברוך הוא טבע כל אדם בחותמו של אדם הראשון - ואין אחד מהן דומה לחבירו. לפיכך כל אחד ואחד חייב לומר : בשבילי נברא העולם.

If a person makes many coins from one mold, they are all exactly alike. But even though God has fashioned every person in the stamp of the first human, not a single one of them is exactly like another.

(Talmud Bavli, Sanhedrin 37a)

Although we were all formed from the same "mold," we are each individuals, and unique. We share similarities but we are also distinct. We are all connected through our commonalities, but we are also

all individuals through our differences.

in·di·vid·u·al·i·ty [in-duh-vij-oo-al-i-tee] *noun*
The particular characteristics or qualities that distinguish one person from others

con·form·i·ty [kuhn-fawr-mi-tee] *noun*
Congruence; action in accord with prevailing social standards, attitudes, practices, etc.

We walk a fine line between individuality and conformity. Both are important for different reasons, and both serve an important purpose in our lives. For example, let's take being Jewish. As a Jew, you belong to the Jewish community; on a small scale, your USY community, and on the largest scale, the entire Jewish nation. As a member of the Jewish community, you ascribe to a certain set of shared beliefs (like belief in God), values (like *tikun olam*), and practices (having a bar or bat mitzvah). At the same time, you are still an individual. You have the ability to decide how you are going to live your life as a Jew within this community.

Activity: All My Hats

What are the different roles I play? What different "hats" do I wear that make me who I am? Fill in the hats with different pieces of you.

Look back at the pie you made to represent the various communities you are part of in Part One of the sourcebook. Choose the group you feel is your "primary" community (or at least one of your primary communities), and think about the following:

- *How are you similar to other people in that group?*
- *How are you different than other people in that group?*
- *Take a look at the definition for conformity—are there standards, attitudes or practices that distinguish that group from another? Do you behave, dress or talk in a certain way that is specific to that group?*
- *Can you be an individual and still conform to the standards of a group?*

Earlier, we used this text to talk about the importance of community. Now, let's look at it through the lens of the individual versus the group:

הִלֵּל אוֹמֵר, אַל תִּפְרוֹשׁ מִן הַצִּבּוּר ...וְאַל תָּדִין אֶת חֲבֵרְךָ עַד שֶׁתַּגִּיעַ לִמְקוֹמוֹ

Hillel says: Don't separate yourself from the community... and don't judge your friend until you have put yourself in his place.

(Pirkei Avot 2:4)

How does Hillel express both the importance of the community and the importance of the individual in his statement?

Clearly, being part of a community is important however, the individual is important too. If we were all the same, why would someone need to look at things from the perspective of another?

Activity: Someone else's shoes

Consider a recent argument you had with a friend or family member. Take a minute to describe the argument to a friend.

Now tell the story as if you were speaking from the other person's perspective.

Did telling the story of the other person's perspective help you understand his/her perspective? How can we learn to understand someone else, learn different perspectives and practice being there for one another?

ז וַיִּיצֶר יְהוָה אֱלֹהִים אֶת-הָאָדָם, עָפָר מִן-הָאֲדָמָה, וַיִּפַּח בְּאַפָּיו, נִשְׁמַת חַיִּים; וַיְהִי הָאָדָם, לְנֶפֶשׁ חַיָּה.

7 Then the Lord God formed man of the dust of the ground, and breathed into his nostrils the breath of life; and man became a living soul.

(Bereishit 2:7)

We see from the above texts that every person is made up of two parts—*Adam*, or man, which was made from the dust of the earth, and *neshama*, soul, which God breathed into each of us. Both body and soul are important components to a person; one can not exist without the other. If we look at the Hebrew words for body and soul, *Adam* is a masculine term, and *neshama* is a feminine term. Just like each person has both physical and spiritual parts, every person also has both "feminine" and "masculine" attributes.

Ying and Yang, "Mini-Me, you complete me"
Let's look again at the text from Bereishit 2:18:

יח וַיֹּאמֶר יְהוָה אֱלֹהִים, לֹא-טוֹב הֱיוֹת הָאָדָם לְבַדּוֹ; אֶעֱשֶׂה-לּוֹ עֵזֶר, כְּנֶגְדּוֹ.

18 It is not good for man to be alone; I will make a fitting helper for him.

(Bereishit 2:18)

In the movie series *Austin Powers*, Dr. Evil tells his sidekick Mini-Me, that he "completes him." Do you think this source of laughter is rooted in the biblical text from Bereishit? Do the partners in a healthy relationship truly complete each other? How?

A glimpse into another culture: In the Chinese concept of Ying and Yang there are two separate energies or forces (often opposites) that interact to form one complete circle. Compare this concept to that of a healthy partnership. Can you think of any Ying and Yang in your life? Ying and Yang demonstrate equality and completeness between two separate entities, just as the Bereishit text describes man and woman as two separate entities coming from one whole.

Activity: Ying and Yang
Think of one person who complements your character – who best fits the "Ying" to your "Yang" or is best fit as your "*ezer k'negdo*" or "partner in crime." It could be a best friend, a significant other, a parent, your brother or sister, anyone you feel truly understands and "completes" you!

Draw out a Ying Yang design and fill in each space with character traits that balance your relationship as one of equality, dignity and mutual respect

Gender Stereotypes

Eve was created as Adam's partner such that each of them complemented the traits the other lacked. Are there specific "male" or "female" traits that make one whole? Do man and woman complete each other or are complementary traits only based on gender stereotypes?

Gender stereotypes can inhibit people from being their best selves and fulfilling their own ambitions. Stepping outside the norms of society's ideas of what it means to be a man or a woman may feel uncomfortable, but it is more important to be true to ourselves than to conform.

Activity: Act Like a Man/ Act Like a Lady

In the boxes below, write any attributes, behaviors or emotions you think are generally attributed to either men or women.

Think about high-profile characters in the media. Is there a person you can think of who exemplifies a "real man" or a "real lady?" Add them into the box.

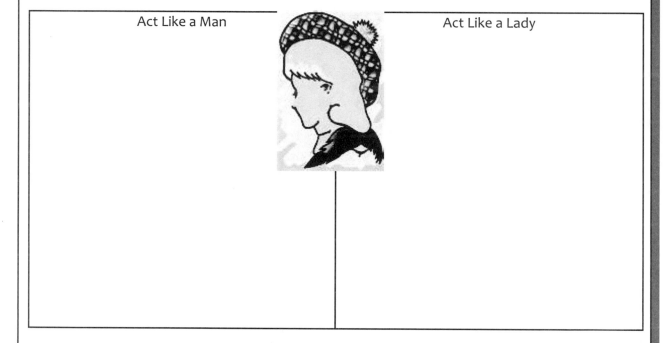

Act Like a Man

Act Like a Lady

Do the boxes you created describe a typical boy and typical girl? Why or why not?
Are boys and girls born into the "roles" you have described in your boxes?
If we are not born this way, why do you think attributes, behaviors and emotions are more commonly attributed to one gender over another?

(Activity adapted from Paul Kivel. Men's Work: How to Stop the Violence That Tears Our Lives Apart. 1992, rev. 1998, Used with Permission.)

Activity: Be Professional

For each profession below, mark whether your first thought is to imagine a male or a female in that role by circling the male 🧍 or female 🧍 icon next to the word:

🧍 🧍 Doctor   🧍 🧍 Receptionist

🧍 🧍 Lawyer   🧍 🧍 Senator

🧍 🧍 Construction worker 🧍 🧍 Computer technician

🧍 🧍 Nurse   🧍 🧍 Dentist

🧍 🧍 Banker   🧍 🧍 Teacher

🧍 🧍 Mechanic   🧍 🧍 Babysitter

🧍 🧍 Journalist   🧍 🧍 Author

🧍 🧍 Judge

Were there any professions that were easily definable as male or female? Why?

Were there any professions that were difficult to attribute to one gender? Why?

Why do you think we attribute things like professions to one gender over the other?

What are stereotypes?

A stereotype is a generalization about a group of people, where we attribute a defined set of characteristics to that group. Stereotypes can be positive or negative, and can have both positive and negative impact.

Are the boxes on the previous page stereotypes?
Think about the boxes you created. Do you fit into one of them? Why or why not?
What happens when a boy or girl does not conform but chooses to act in a way that is outside these boxes?

If a boy acts "outside the box," someone may call him a _____.
If a girl acts "outside the box," someone may call her a _____.

Do you think it is easier for girls or boys to step outside the box?
How does name-calling "punish" those who step outside the box?

Scenario 1:

Alyssa and Jon are both running for regional president. They've been dating for five months. They've both served on their regional general boards and are equally qualified. Some people tell Alyssa that she should run for a different position and not compete with Jon. Her mother, who really likes Jon and wants the two of them to keep dating, tells Alyssa that if she wins, Jon will break up with her. Her best friend tells Alyssa that she is threatening to Jon. Alyssa notices that no one tells Jon not to run for the position.

What should Alyssa do?
What should Jon do?
How can Alyssa respond to her mother and her friend?
What do you think will happen to the relationship if Alyssa wins?
What do you think will happen if she doesn't?
If Alyssa backs down and doesn't run, what stereotype is she perpetuating?

Scenario 2:

Becca is 15 years old and is really attracted to Jake. She wants to ask him to hang out with her after school. One day after math class, Becca asks Jake if he'd like to meet her after school. Jake is secretly thrilled but he is afraid that his friends will make fun of him because a girl asked him out.

Did Becca do anything wrong? What should Jake do?

Scenario 3:

Becca and Jake wind up at MoonDollars, a local coffee shop. Since Becca asked Jake out, she wants to pay for his drink. Jake thinks he should pay since he is the boy.

What should they do?

I can counteract stereotypes by _____

How can gender roles affect relationships?

Gender roles can be barriers to fulfilling our individual potential. They prescribe the way we should act and behave. The Conservative Movement recognizes this and has taken strong positions on gender equality. For example, although traditionally only men were permitted to receive ordination and become rabbis, the Conservative movement began ordaining women rabbis nearly 25 years ago. Although traditionally, only men were permitted to wear tefillin and tallitot, it is perfectly acceptable and even encouraged for women within the Conservative movement to wear these ritual items. Many in the Conservative movement embrace the concept of egalitarianism as a permissible option, which can break down many of the preconceived ideas about the roles of men and women.

In this chapter we discussed partnership, conformity and gender roles. Healthy relationships allow us to maintain our individuality while being cooperative and supportive. While we acknowledge that there are differences between men and women, gender roles should never serve to diminish our aspirations to be who we want to be. Males and females should be viewed as equals, as partners and as each being a whole being.

Chapter Four

R·e·s·p·e·c·t— Find out what it means to me

In this chapter we will discuss the concept of respect as it applies to our relationships. Because we are all created in God's image, each of us is entitled to respect and Is obligated to respect other people. There is a special obligation to respect our parents and teachers. Respect is the basis for any relationship, whether it is a friendship or a dating relationship. The objectification of women and men in the media disregards this central precept by portraying them purely as sexual beings. The goals of the chapter are to understand that concepts of respect and dignity are central to Jewish thought and are critical aspects of a healthy relationship, and to start to become media literate.

Let's take a look back at the text about the creation of Man and Woman:

וַיִּבְרָא אֱלֹהִים | אֶת־הָאָדָם בְּצַלְמוֹ בְּצֶלֶם אֱלֹהִים בָּרָא אֹתוֹ זָכָר וּנְקֵבָה בָּרָא אֹתָם

And God created Adam in **God's image**, in the image of God, God created him, male and female God created them.

(Bereishit 1:27)

What does it mean that God created people "in God's image?"

How does this idea impact how we act toward one another?

Many understand this statement to mean that every person is created with a little spark of Godliness; each person is unique, but also connected through this spark.

If each person has a spark of God in them, then every person deserves to be treated with respect and dignity. This concept of *b'tzelem Elohim* has many applications—it motivates us to look beyond a person's exterior to what is inside; it is a call to action for us to engage in social justice to help those less fortunate; and it should be the driving force behind our interactions with others.

שוב מעשה בנכרי אחד שבא לפני שמאי, אמר לו : גיירני על מנת שתלמדני כל התורה כולה כשאני עומד על רגל אחת. דחפו באמת הבנין שבידו. בא לפני הלל, גייריה. אמר לו : דעלך סני לחברך לא תעביד - זו היא כל התורה כולה, ואידך - פירושה הוא, זיל גמור

A non-Jew came before Shammai and requested, "Convert me on condition that you teach me the entire Torah while I stand on one foot." He [Shammai] pushed him out with the ruler in his hand. He [the non-Jew] then came before Hillel, who converted him. Hillel addressed to him the immortal words, "That which is hateful to you, do not do to your fellow. That is the entire Torah; the rest is commentary. Go and learn."

(Talmud Bavli Shabbat 31a)

What do you think of Hillel's summary?
If you were asked to summarize the Torah, what would you say?

Hillel ends his statement with "go and learn." Hillel is not saying that Judaism is just about being nice to people, but he is saying that the foundation of Jewish identity and learning is being a good person. Clearly the person still has to learn all of the mitzvot, but treating others with respect and being a good friend is the basis for many of them.

Activity:
List as many mitzvot as you can that command us to be respectful to others.

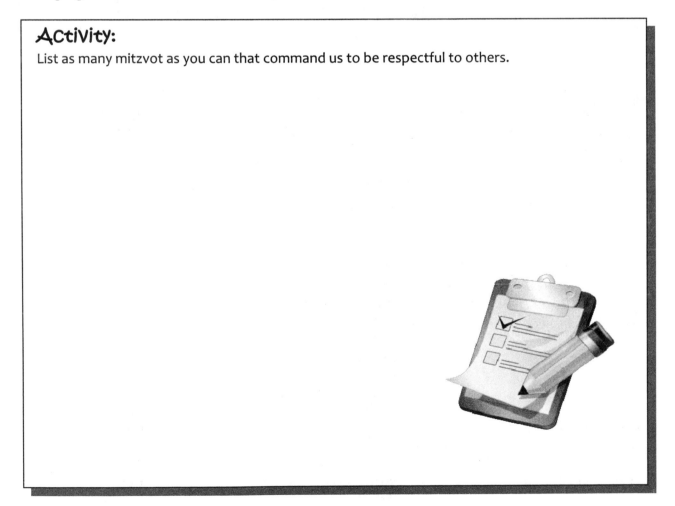

Objectification versus Respect

"Even as a melody is not composed of tones, nor a verse of words, nor a statue of lines—one must pull and tear to turn a unity into a multiplicity—so it is with the human being to whom I say You. I can abstract from him the color of his hair or the color of his speech or the color of his graciousness; I have to do this again and again; but immediately he is no longer You."

—Martin Buber, *I and Thou*

Martin Buber's I and Thou *presents a philosophy of personal dialogue, in that it describes how personal dialogue can define the nature of reality. Buber's major theme is that human existence may be defined by the way in which we engage in dialogue with each other, with the world, and with God. Martin Buber (1878-1965) was one of the 20th century's most widely influential Jewish thinkers. His work included a new translation of the Bible into German, begun with Franz Rosenzweig, and books on interpreting the Bible, on Hasidism, and on many aspects of the philosophy of Judaism.*

What is this excerpt about?

Buber is differentiating between two different ways of looking at relationships—an "I—You" relationship, and an "I—it" relationship. When we categorize people by color, religion, sexual orientation, etc. we make them less than they are. We break someone into "pieces," so we are now looking at an "it" as opposed to a person, a "you."

An "I—it" relationship with another person can be dangerous. When we turn someone into an "it," with no opinions or feelings, we run the risk of treating that person with disrespect. After all, would you treat your shoe with the same respect that you treat your friend?

Throughout history, the forces of evil have tried to tell us that the spark of Godliness is only granted to some people, and not others. During the Holocaust, Hitler convinced a good part of the world that Jews, Gypsies, people who are gay, and people who were physically and/or mentally disabled, were not people, they did not have that spark, and were therefore undeserving of respect or dignity. Still, in many parts of the world today, the lack of respect and dignity for others leads to acts of aggression and violence.

The way others perceive us or define us, often with lack of respect or dignity, leads to objectification. In Western cultures, the objectification of both women and men is often a result of media influence.

Media Literacy

"American children and adolescents spend 22 to 28 hours per week viewing television, more than any other activity except sleeping. By the age of 70 they will have spent 7 to 10 years of their lives watching TV." —- The Kaiser Family Foundation

Entertainment media often portray people solely as sexual objects rather than as whole people. In this section we will deconstruct some entertainment media in order to understand their effects on women and men. Becoming media literate will help us analyze the images and words of the media and understand their core messages. By critically assessing and evaluating these images and words, we can better understand the impact of media and choose to take meaningful action to stop the spread of these messages. While we are unable to include specific ads, music or videos in this sourcebook, you can analyze ads in nearly any magazine, listen and watch nearly any music video and listen to nearly any popular song and find images, whether verbal or pictorial, that portray women and men as objects rather than as people.

Activity: The Messages behind the Media

Many advertisements in magazines, on billboards and on TV encourage us to think about people in parts instead of as whole persons. Open up a magazine and look at the ads, pay attention the next time you are watching a show on TV. Are there parts of men or women that are emphasized? Are there ads that only show parts instead of the whole? Does race or gender play a role in the way in which the "parts" are emphasized? Is the lure of sex being used to sell products? Are these ads respectful to women? Are they respectful to men? What do you think some of the consequences are of seeing these ads all the time?

I notice that in ads that depict women, these parts of the whole are emphasized:

_____

I notice that in ads that depict men, these parts of the whole are emphasized:

_____

Were the parts emphasized the same for men and women?
Did you notice any themes in the ads?
Are any particular stereotypes or gender generalizations perpetuated in the media?
What about racial generalizations?

Do the magazines you selected use photos of people who realistically represent the general public?

Do they use photos of models or do they use photos of real people? If they use photos of real people, in what parts of the magazine can they be found:
  ° The cover?
  ° Advertisements?
  ° Beauty/Style Sections?
  ° Content? (photos that accompany the articles)

Can any implications be made if the photos in the magazine articles are of average people while the photos in advertisements are models?

What is the main message of the magazine?

Does the magazine promote independence, or does it reinforce the idea that young people should be more concerned with looks, relationships and the approval of others?

Do the physical ideals represented in this magazine reflect reality? Who is not represented here?

Do the topics explored in this magazine reflect the real concerns of young people?

Create a profile of a 'typical 'young person, based on the content of this magazine. Is this an accurate profile of someone in real life?

The media capitalize on stereotypes that perpetuate disrespect and inequality by idealizing particular images and building off of stereotypes. Advertisements and commercials rarely depict the "average Jane", but rather an image of an overly perfect body. What the consumer does not recognize is the amount of "fake-up," "artwork" or airbrushing that is applied to a cover shot or photo - shoot. When the media constantly surround us with these images, it can affect us in the most subconscious of ways, leading to issues with low self-esteem, eating disorders, self-disgust and body image issues, or worse. Boys and girls, men and women, may think that they (as a creation of God) are not "good enough" because they do not look like the people on their TV screens and in the magazines they read. The effect of this is perhaps more damaging than we can even understand. Research shows that the images of violence and domination are internalized by us, even to the point where we begin to treat others disrespectfully. Men who are typically portrayed as being powerful, may make young boys and teens think that they need to be powerful and domineering. If girls and women are seen exclusively as sexual beings rather than complicated people with many interests, talents, and identities, boys and men may have difficulty relating to them on any level other than sexual.

Describe the picture according to the following concepts:

The effects of the media on the human image—how the media alters a natural creation of God to send a particular message

Self esteem and self perception- why is it that we can't always see the "lion" within us?

It is important to remember that the messages we receive from the media are ones to be taken with a grain of salt. The media use techniques to send both obvious and subliminal messages and play with one's conscious. What you see isn't what you get. The media should never be used as a teaching tool for how we relate to others, or how we understand ourselves; rather it is only people and our relationships with them that can help us understand the way to healthy relationships.

Activity: Popular Music

Select three popular songs about relationships and listen to each. Write down all the words used to describe the woman in each song. Then write down all the ways used to describe the guy in each song. Circle all the body parts and sexual feelings in red marker. Circle all the emotions in blue. What color are most of the circles? How would you describe the relationships in the songs? What are they based on? How do the people relate to each other? Are these relationships based on respect and equality? What common words are used as synonyms for women? What words are used to describe men? What is the issue with using these words as song lyrics?

Do you know any song lyrics that can promote positive messages of respect and dignity for others? What about for the self?

If media determine the messages we receive about how we regard others as well as ourselves, how can we overcome the negative messages we're bombarded with every day and learn to respect all living things?

Respect in Relationships

אֵיזֶהוּ מְכֻבָּד, הַמְכַבֵּד אֶת הַבְּרִיּוֹת, שֶׁנֶּאֱמַר (שמואל א ב), כִּי מְכַבְּדַי אֲכַבֵּד וּבֹזַי יֵקָלּוּ :

Who is respected? One who honors his fellows, as it is written (I Shmuel 2:30), "Those who honor Me, I will honor; but those who scorn me will be despised."

(Pirkei Avot 4:1)

- *How do we respect others?*
- *How does one gain respect? Lose it?*
- *Why is (mutual) respect so critical in a friendship or relationship?*

R-E-S-P-E-C-T: Find out what it means to me

Define respect on your own terms. What does it mean to treat someone else with respect? How does being treated with respect feel? How does it feel to be disrespected? Do you appreciate respect more so when it's taken from you?

What are some ways we disrespect each other, intentionally or unintentionally?

We disrespect others through words by _____.

We disrespect others through actions by _____.

> Rabbi Akiva had twelve thousand pairs of students
> and all of them died in one period because
> they were lacking in respect toward each other.
> (Talmud Yevamot 62b)

What can we learn from this text?

Derech Eretz, translated here as "appropriate behavior" is the title of two shorter tractates in the Talmud:

> Derech Eretz Rabbah, which describes rules by illustrating personal stories of our sages and Derech Eretz Zutah, which describes ethical teachings, rules of conduct and the ethics of behavior. Since Jewish Law guides us down a path for ethical living, derech eretz is then a central Jewish value.

Define: Derech Eretz

Derech Eretz literally means "the way of the land," and is interpreted to mean appropriate and respectful behavior. Check off which words would best define Derech Eretz

- ☐ Dignity
- ☐ Courtesy
- ☐ Ethical behavior
- ☐ Respect
- ☐ Way
- ☐ Rules
- ☐ Fair, equal

Activity: "The way" or "Derech"

Along the path put labels of "derech eretz" such as derech eretz at school, derech eretz on the basketball team, derech eretz at home, etc.

Mark each "derech" by writing examples of how you demonstrate respectful, appropriate behavior on it. What types of behavior are the same no matter where you are? What behaviors are appropriate in some places and not in others?

Activity: Rank Your Actions

Ethical actions: Rank in order, what determines your behavior when making choices to behave with dignity and respect (derech eretz):

You see something that challenges your morals. When deciding what to do, your consideration is:

- ☐ What will the others think of me? Maybe if they're calling him a "loser," they'll think I'm a loser too.
- ☐ I don't want to be in his place so I'm going to stay out of it
- ☐ It's just not cool
- ☐ This has nothing to do with me, it's none of my business
- ☐ I don't want to be outcast
- ☐ I'm trying to protect my image/reputation and this isn't going to help it

Language and Respect

We will look further at the issue of language and respect in Chapter Seven. But let's consider how our language can indicate respect.

Feelings of love and respect can fluctuate with frustration and discontent, often resulting in our using the word "hate" toward those we are meant to genuinely respect. Have you ever screamed "I hate you!" to your parent(s)? Do you sometimes feel challenged to respect your parents? What about a teacher who continuously makes your life stressful with homework?

Activity: Watch What You Say

Look at the phrases below and circle the ones you use.

"Urgh, you're driving me crazy"
"But Mom....."
"Shut up, you're annoying me"
"stop bugging me"
"I'll do it later"
Chill!

Or teachers:
"this is dumb"
"what's the point"
"I'm not doing this"
"But I didn't do anything!"

Think of other ways to say the same thing: Instead of _____, I can try and say_____.

- *How do you talk to your parents? Your friends? Your teachers?*
- *Would you use the same language with your grandparents or do you treat them with more respect?*
- *Do you treat your teachers with less or more respect than your parents? Do you use appropriate words? Do you disagree respectfully?*
- *How can you learn to communicate respectfully while still sharing your feelings with both parents and teachers?*
- **If you show your parents and teachers respect, they in turn will most likely respect you. Growing up in respectful relationships gives you a model for how to act respectfully in other relationships. Your own household will be one in which everyone respects each other and you, your partner and children will feel loved, valued, and safe.**

Aside from language, what are some other ways we can show our respect for our parents and teachers? What about doing what our parents ask of us without arguing or procrastinating? How does that show respect? What type of atmosphere does it create when we are respectful to our parents and teachers?

Have you ever seen someone get up from his or her seat when a parent or teacher enters the room? That is one way that some people show respect for these figures. If you've ever seen the President, Prime Minister or someone of similar stature enter the room, you may have noticed that everyone rises. Why do they do that?

On another level, consider the choreography of Jewish prayer. We stand to approach God for the *Amidah*, we stand when we recite the Mourner's *Kaddish*, we stand when we call the community to prayer in the *Barchu.* Why?

Earlier, we talked about how throughout history, people have tried to dehumanize others by dividing them into parts, so they are less than human, lacking that divine and Godly spark. Another way to dehumanize people is to call them names that make them seem unworthy of respect, and sometimes, not even human at all. For example, Hitler called the Jews "rats" and "demons," and compared the Jewish people to a "disease" from which the German people needed to be "cured." Similarly, during the 1994 genocide in Rwanda, the Hutu aggressors called the Tutsis, and any Hutus who sympathized with the Tutsis and wanted peace, "cockroaches."

What kind of impact did using these derogatory terms have during the Holocaust and the Rwandan genocide? Can you think of words we use that disrespect others, even if we don't mean them to do so?

Some disrespectful words we use are:

_____   _____   _____

_____   _____   _____

Are there other words we can use in place of these disrespectful ones?

_____   _____   _____

_____   _____   _____

How can those disrespectful words impact how we think about and act toward others?

In this chapter we learned that respecting one another is central to any healthy relationship. We show respect in many ways, including our language, our actions, and by refusing to objectify people, by treating each as a unique individual created in the image of God. Since popular music, advertisements and other media often choose to objectify people we must be aware of the disrespectful ways in which men and women are depicted and not let that affect our own relationships, the ways we engage with other people or view ourselves. We have also noted by studying history, how disrespect and dehumanization can lead to horrific consequences such as the genocides suffered by our own people in the Holocaust and more recently in Rwanda and Darfur. The mass level consequences start with the individual. You have the power to make a difference in how you treat others with kindness and respect.

Chapter Five
our Bodies, our souls

Before we can continue our discussion about interpersonal relationships, we need to look further at the concept of respecting ourselves. Before we can respect others, we need to first have self respect.

Our bodies and souls are holy and it is our duty to maintain that holiness through modesty in our dress, speech, and activity, and taking care of our bodies and souls. Sexual relations are also holy and an important part of a committed relationship so long as both people desire and consent to the relations. However, there is a great deal of pressure on teens to engage in sexual activity, and the media tends to debase sexual activity while at the same time putting pressure on teens to engage in it.

---

7 And God formed the human from dust of the earth, and God blew the soul of life into it.

(Bereishit 2:7)

ז וַיִּיצֶר יְהוָה אֱלֹהִים אֶת-הָאָדָם, עָפָר מִן-הָאֲדָמָה, וַיִּפַּח בְּאַפָּיו, נִשְׁמַת חַיִּים; וַיְהִי הָאָדָם, לְנֶפֶשׁ חַיָּה.

We discussed earlier the concept that all mitzvot deal with relationships – either the relationship between a person and God, between a person and another person, between a person and the environment and of course between a person and himself or herself. This last category, known in Hebrew as *mitzvot* that are *bein adam l'atzmo* are mitzvot dealing with one of the most sacred relationships —the relationship you have with yourself.

Earlier, we talked about how God created each person from two types of "material"—from the dust of the earth, He created a physical body (*guf*), and from God's own "breath," God blew life in the form of a spiritual soul (*neshama*) into each of us.

Both parts of our being, our body and our soul, are important. We cannot live just as a soul without a body, and we cannot live as an empty physical shell without a soul. It is our responsibility to take care of both our *guf* and our *neshama*.

Many commentaries say that we are "borrowing" our bodies from God, since a soul cannot exist without a body. Are you more careful with something that belongs to you, or something that belongs to someone else?

I keep my body healthy by: _____

What about keeping our soul and our internal self healthy?_____

_____

We may think a lot about keeping our physical bodies healthy—eating a healthy diet, exercising, playing sports, even showering keeps our bodies healthy. Just as we feed and take care of our body, we must do the same for our soul. Our body allows our soul to exist in the world, but our soul is what makes each of us unique and special. Bodies have two hands, two feet, two eyes, one nose, and so on—but our souls are as different as they can be. As we discussed previously in the section on individuality, we each have our own personality quirks and eccentricities, likes and dislikes.

Activity: I Am Unique ...

I am good at _____
Some things that make me happy are: _____
Some things that make me sad are: _____
If I could change one thing in the world it would be:

_____
My secret ambition is to: _____

Compare these answers with a friend's. What do you have in common? What is different? What makes you unique?

רַבִּי אוֹמֵר, אַל תִּסְתַּכֵּל בַּקַּנְקַן, אֶלָּא בַּמֶּה שֶׁיֶּשׁ בּוֹ.

Do not look at the vessel, rather what is inside.
(Pirkei Avot 4:20)

Is it harder to look at the "outside" or the "inside" of a person? Why?

"Don't judge a book by its cover"- but we do!

External characteristics like facial features, skin color and height are the first thing you notice about a person because that's the first thing you see. But to determine whether a person is kind or unkind takes a different type of looking.

Why do you think your parents care if your skirt is too short or if your jeans are ripped or your hair is messy, too long or not brushed nicely? The reality is that most people do "judge a book by its cover" whether you like it or not!

Even the most righteous person can mistakenly judge someone by outward appearance. Samuel the Prophet makes such a mistake when God sends him to anoint a new king:

ו וַיְהִי בְּבוֹאָם, וַיַּרְא אֶת-אֱלִיאָב; וַיֹּאמֶר, אַךְ נֶגֶד יְהוָה מְשִׁיחוֹ.

6 When they arrived and he saw Eliab, he [Samuel] thought: "Surely the Lord's anointed stands before Him."

ז וַיֹּאמֶר יְהוָה אֶל-שְׁמוּאֵל, אַל-תַּבֵּט אֶל-מַרְאֵהוּ וְאֶל-גְּבֹהַּ קוֹמָתוֹ--כִּי מְאַסְתִּיהוּ: כִּי לֹא, אֲשֶׁר יִרְאֶה הָאָדָם--כִּי הָאָדָם יִרְאֶה לַעֵינַיִם, וַיהוָה יִרְאֶה לַלֵּבָב.

7 But God said to Samuel: "Pay no attention to his appearance or his stature, for I have rejected him. For God does not see how people see; a person sees only what is visible, but God sees what is in the heart."

(I Shmuel 16:6-7)

Seven of Jesse's sons pass before Samuel, but each time, God rejects him.

יא וַיֹּאמֶר שְׁמוּאֵל אֶל-יִשַׁי, הֲתַמּוּ הַנְּעָרִים, וַיֹּאמֶר עוֹד שָׁאַר הַקָּטָן, וְהִנֵּה רֹעֶה בַּצֹּאן; וַיֹּאמֶר שְׁמוּאֵל אֶל-יִשַׁי שִׁלְחָה וְקָחֶנּוּ, כִּי לֹא-נָסֹב עַד-בֹּאוֹ פֹה.

11 Then Samuel asked Jesse: "Are these all the boys you have?" He [Jesse] replied: "There is still the youngest [David]; he is tending the flock"... And Samuel said to Jesse: 'Send and fetch him; for we will not sit down till he comes here.'

יב וַיִּשְׁלַח וַיְבִיאֵהוּ וְהוּא אַדְמוֹנִי, עִם-יְפֵה עֵינַיִם וְטוֹב רֹאִי;

12 So they sent and brought him. He was ruddy-cheeked with pretty eyes, and handsome. And God said: "Rise and anoint him, for this is the one."

(I Shmuel 16:11-12)

Why does Samuel make this mistake?
After what God tells Samuel, why do you think the text still describes David by his outward appearance?
How does the idea of not judging by outward appearance connect to the idea of judging each person favorably- dan l'kaf zechut- which we discussed in the chapter on friendship?

Perception of others, perception of self

You want others to look at you and think positively. Can others see you positively if you don't necessarily see yourself that way?

God is like a mirror. The mirror never changes but everyone who sees it, sees a different face. A thousand may look at it and it reflects each of them. Thus, the text does not say: "I the Lord am your God," addressed to the collective, but "I the Lord am your God" addressed to the individual.

"God's mirror is one, but the reflections in it are many. Each one of us looks into God's mirror and sees a particular individual reflection of God"

Ron Wolfson, "God's To Do List: 103 Ways to be an Angel and do God's Work on Earth," Jewish Lights Publishing, 2006, page 8

Self Perception: an exercise

Quiz time: How long does it take you to pick out what you're going to wear to school each morning? What do you think about when choosing what clothing to buy, or what to wear to school? Do you think about how others will look at you? When you look at yourself in a mirror, what's the first thing you see? What do you not see?

Activity: Mirror, Mirror on the Wall

Imagine you are sitting in front of a mirror. What do you see about yourself? Use the "mirror" below to draw, write or cut and paste magazine pictures to describe what you see,

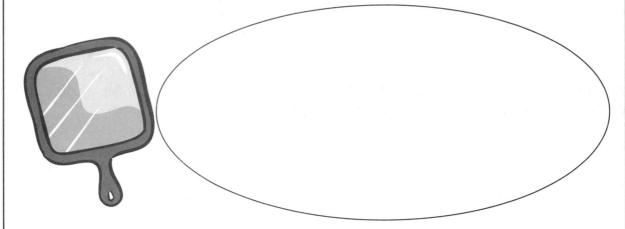

Now, pretend you are looking in a mirror that reflects not your outside self, but your inside self. What do you see? Use the "mirror" below to draw or write what you see.

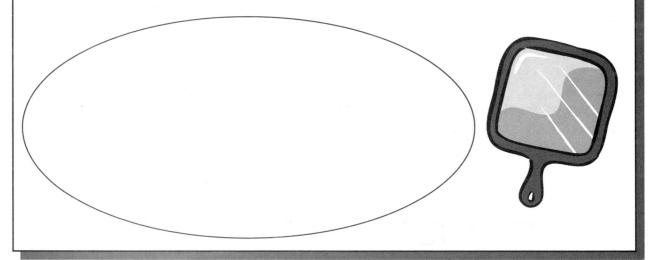

- *Why do we pay so much attention to our "outside" if the "inside" is what counts?*
- *What are the challenges to looking past a person's "outside" to see the "inside?"*
- *What are some ways to overcome those challenges?*

Image is Everything: The Manly Man, the Girly Girl

Fill in the blanks:

A girl's body should be _____

A guy's body should be _____

The first thing I notice about a girl I am attracted to is _____

The first thing I notice about a guy I am attracted to is: _____

Why is our society so obsessed with physical perfection? Doesn't God create us each uniquely for a reason? What is that reason?

ב דַּבֵּר אֶל-כָּל-עֲדַת בְּנֵי-יִשְׂרָאֵל, וְאָמַרְתָּ אֲלֵהֶם—קְדֹשִׁים תִּהְיוּ: כִּי קָדוֹשׁ, אֲנִי יְהוָה אֱלֹהֵיכֶם.

2 Speak to all the congregation of the children of Israel, and say unto them: You shall be holy; for I the Lord your God am holy.

(Vayikra 19:2)

Parashat Kedoshim, in the book of Vayikra, is dedicated to Moshe telling the people about many of God's commandments. The above statement is the preface to this section of Torah.

- How does this statement set the tone for the rest of the parasha?
- What does it mean to be kadosh, or holy?
- How does this relate to the concept of b'tzelem Elohim?
- Are we inherently kadosh, or do we make our selves kadosh (or not kadosh)?

I am holy through my actions by _____

I am holy through my words by _____

What do males think about their bodies?

Body Image is not only a "girl thing." Guys too, scrutinize themselves when they look in a mirror. Male body image is rarely discussed, but it is real and plagues the minds of males as well as females.

Activity: Males—Myths and Facts

Answer the True or False question and read the follow-up fact

1. When I look at a sports or fitness magazine, I compare the images I see to my own body

        True   or   *False*

Fact: Western Society promotes an idealized male body through media and cultural "norms

2. I have tried a specific diet to alter my body (i.e. high protein, low calorie, low carb)

        True   or   *False*

Fact: Seventeen percent of men are dieting at any given time

3. I go to the gym to "beef up." No girl wants to date a scrawny guy

        True   or   *False*

Fact: Although exercise is to be encouraged as a healthy habit, 20% of regular exercisers are addicted to exercise either physically or mentally

4. There is nothing wrong with taking something to "help" my muscles grow

        True   or   *False*

Fact: 3.5% (10th grade) or 4% (12th grade) males abuse steroids or muscle enhancing drugs.

Anyone claiming that men aren't concerned with their body image is denying these facts and the influence of the media on both men and women. Other causes of negative male body image include:

- Teasing (for being too thin, too weak or too fat).
- Peer pressure among teenage boys to be tough and strong.
- A cultural tendency to judge people on their appearance.
- Advertising campaigns and media coverage featuring idealized male images.
- Promotion by society of the ideal man as always being strong, lean and muscular
- Well-meaning public health campaigns that urge people to lose weight.
- The emphasis on male sports players as role models for boys.

Respect for Our Bodies

One way that we acknowledge our *kedusha*, our holiness, is through the way we treat our bodies. Although many commentaries say that our bodies are just vessels for our souls, it is still very important to treat our bodies with respect, and care for them.

Parshat Kedoshim prohibits us from making changes to our bodies, out of respect for how God created us.

כח וְשֶׂרֶט לָנֶפֶשׁ, לֹא תִתְּנוּ בִּבְשַׂרְכֶם, וּכְתֹבֶת קַעֲקַע, לֹא תִתְּנוּ בָּכֶם: אֲנִי, יְהוָה.

28 You shall not make gashes in your flesh for the dead, or incise any marks on yourselves.
(Vayikra 19:28)

The "gashes" refer to a sign of mourning; certain cultures would make cuts in their flesh in order to show that they were mourning the death of a love one. In Judaism, traditions of mourning include tearing a piece of clothing rather than cutting our bodies.

Most commentaries define "incise any marks on yourself" as tattoos, and piercings that are not "prevailing local custom." With regard to tattoos, this prohibition was most likely based on a pagan ritual, as were many prohibitions at the time. Although there is no pagan imagery associated with tattoos anymore, it remains a taboo.

Piercings present an interesting discussion because it is clear in the Torah that both men and women wore earrings and nose rings in ancient times:

ב וַיֹּאמֶר אֲלֵהֶם, אַהֲרֹן, פָּרְקוּ נִזְמֵי הַזָּהָב, אֲשֶׁר בְּאָזְנֵי נְשֵׁיכֶם בְּנֵיכֶם וּבְנֹתֵיכֶם; וְהָבִיאוּ, אֵלָי.

2 Aaron said to them: "Take off the gold rings that are on the ears of your wives, your sons and your daughters, and bring them to me.

ג וַיִּתְפָּרְקוּ, כָּל-הָעָם, אֶת-נִזְמֵי הַזָּהָב, אֲשֶׁר בְּאָזְנֵיהֶם; וַיָּבִיאוּ, אֶל-אַהֲרֹן.

3 And all the people took off the gold rings that were in their ears and brought them to Aaron. This he took from them and cast in a mold, and made it into a molten calf.
(Shmot 32:2-3)

Today, excessive piercings in areas that are not normally seen or in socially unacceptable areas are discouraged.

How have societal guidelines about clothing, piercings and accessories changed over time?

Tzniut- Modesty

Another way we are kadosh and show respect for our bodies is through *tzniut*, or modesty. The concept of *tzinut* is a central component of our own holiness. It requires that we keep all sexual activity private – through the way we dress — never being dressed in a way that is sexually revealing, through the way we speak— not talking about sexual activity or using sexual innuendo in public, and the way we act in public — not conducting any sexual activity in public.
(Excerpted from " This Is My Beloved, This Is My Friend: A Rabbinic Letter on Intimate Relations" by Rabbi Elliot N. Dorff on behalf of the Rabbinical Assembly, page 9)

כא וַיַּפֵּל יְהוָה אֱלֹהִים תַּרְדֵּמָה עַל-הָאָדָם, וַיִּישָׁן; וַיִּקַּח, אַחַת מִצַּלְעֹתָיו, וַיִּסְגֹּר בָּשָׂר, תַּחְתֶּנָּה.

21 And the Lord God caused a deep sleep to fall upon the man, and he slept; and God took one of his ribs, and closed up the place with flesh instead thereof.

כב וַיִּבֶן יְהוָה אֱלֹהִים אֶת-הַצֵּלָע אֲשֶׁר-לָקַח מִן-הָאָדָם, לְאִשָּׁה; וַיְבִאֶהָ, אֶל-הָאָדָם.

22 And the rib, which the Lord God had taken from the man, made God a woman, and brought her unto the man.

כג וַיֹּאמֶר, הָאָדָם, זֹאת הַפַּעַם עֶצֶם מֵעֲצָמַי, וּבָשָׂר מִבְּשָׂרִי; לְזֹאת יִקָּרֵא אִשָּׁה, כִּי מֵאִישׁ לֻקְחָה-זֹּאת.

23 And Adam said, "This is now bone of my bones, and flesh of my flesh; she shall be called Woman, because she was taken out of Man.

כד עַל-כֵּן, יַעֲזָב-אִישׁ, אֶת-אָבִיו, וְאֶת-אִמּוֹ; וְדָבַק בְּאִשְׁתּוֹ, וְהָיוּ לְבָשָׂר אֶחָד.

24 Therefore shall a man leave his father and his mother, and shall cleave to his wife; and they shall be one flesh.

כה וַיִּהְיוּ שְׁנֵיהֶם עֲרוּמִּים, הָאָדָם וְאִשְׁתּוֹ; וְלֹא, יִתְבֹּשָׁשׁוּ.

25 And they were both naked, the man and his wife, and were not ashamed."

(Bereishit 2:21-25)

In Bereishit 2:25, we read that the man and wife were not ashamed. What reason would they have to be ashamed? From whom would they feel shame?

What does modesty mean to you?

Modesty means: **mod·es·ty** [mod-uh-stee] *noun*
Regard for decency of behavior, speech, dress, etc.
Simplicity; moderation.

If we take an expanded look at modesty, *tzniut* means dressing, speaking and behaving in a way that is appropriate to the context or situation, and ensuring that we are sensitive and respectful to others. For example, would you wear a bathing suit to synagogue? This would not be appropriate for its setting, and it would make you stand out in comparison to others around you.

I am modest in how I dress by _____

I am modest in how I speak by _____

I am modest in how I behave by _____

Activity: You are What You Wear

Modesty is much more than covering yourself up or speaking humbly. Modesty will determine what others think about you.

In the left-hand column below list the major articles of clothing or jewelry you are wearing or plan to wear today. In the right-hand column write down what you want your attire to say about you. For example, next to "designer jeans" you might say "Up with the latest style;", "team jackets or chapter t-shirts," or "I want everyone to know what I represent," etc.

Look at your clothing choice for today. Does it reflect what you want people to say/think about you?

What I am wearing	What I want it to say about me

After completing the list, think about the following questions:

Are there certain times you want to convey a different impression?

Do you dress differently for school? Synagogue? Parties? Concerts? Why or why not?

Suppose you were offered someone's wardrobe for free. Whose would you want? Whose would you not accept?

What do the costumes of some popular movie stars, singers or musicians say about their values and how they want to be judged by the audience? And what does that choice of attire say about how they perceive the values of the audience? Is it good for society?

Does the use of unnaturally thin models to display clothing have an impact on our values? Does the claim that the designers want to emphasize the clothes rather than the model make a difference?

They say "clothes don't make the man," but in reality, people are immediately judged by their appearance, including (and especially among teenagers) clothing choices.

One of the issues concerned with dress is what is appropriate dress in various circumstances. Laura Geller, in an article entitled "Modesty is Expressed Many Fashions" questions certain accepted standards and examines some of the relationships between clothing and modesty.

> …What is really meant by modesty in dress? Does it mean that I should not wear a pants suit to work? Does it mean I should not appear on a public beach in a bathing suit? Does it mean that I should cover my hair? Can I wear sleeveless dresses? … Is my body less kadosh in a bathing suit than in a long dress? For me the question is not one of modesty in dress but rather appropriateness in dress…

> …In the area of sexuality, as in the area of dress, the major issue is one of appropriate response. It is appropriate in certain instances to "open up" emotionally, to touch or kiss or be physically intimate. In other situations it is inappropriate. Who is to judge? Each individual should be encouraged to make his/her own decision based on his/her own understanding of the sanctity of personhood.

> Many family arguments have been conducted between parents and children disagreeing as to what was appropriate attire. All too often, for instance, many people looked upon the High Holidays not as an opportunity to reexamine one's own behavior as much as an opportunity to show off one's new clothes. More time was spent on examining the nuances of fashion than may have been spent on the nuances of prayer, behavior, and repentance.
>
> (Sh'ma, vol. 9, no. 162. November 24, 1978 reprinted from B'Tzelem Elohim, United Synagogue Youth,)

Laura Geller raised the question, "who is to judge what is modest and what is appropriate?" She answers that each individual is to make up his/her mind based upon his/her own understanding of the sanctity of personhood.

Develop some arguments of the Jewish tradition for and against this position. Think of what other groups might be considered as having the right to make a decision as to what is appropriate and what is inappropriate. How does one balance a modern desire for individuals to make up their own minds and the classical Jewish tradition which talks about prevailing community standards expressed in halachah (Jewish law).

Should Jews dress in a distinctive fashion? Should Jews dress in such a way that would enable people to tell immediately that an individual is Jewish? Why or why not? What would the consequences be of adopting such a pattern of dress? Has maintaining a distinctive dress style helped the Amish or the Hasidim? How do you feel dressed in modern clothes walking by a Hasid dressed in his distinctive style?

List some of the items that are distinctively Jewish in nature that people can wear to identify themselves as Jews. Discuss the benefits of wearing each of the items listed.

One popular custom in modern times is for Jews to wear a Magen David (Star of David) on a chain around their necks or as some part of other ornamental or functional jewelry. Some people wear a mezuzah on a chain around their necks. One of the reasons given for wearing such items is that Christians often wear a cross and Jews need a similar way to identify themselves. Others just like to let people know that they are Jewish, so they can limit relationships they don't wish to encourage.

Are these reasons valid? Would they be any different for Jews in other cultures?

If you follow such practices, why do you do so, and do they help you in any positive way to relate to your Jewishness? Would this be the case if the Magen David were on a money clip, bagel dish, or other similar items?

Some people may say that the concept of *tzniut* limits self-expression and creates a sense of shame about the body, while others may say that *tzniut* creates a sense of respect for something special.

- **What do you think about the idea of *tzniut*? How would you define the Jewish value of tzniut? Is it all about covering yourself from head-to-toe or is there more to it?**
- **Do you think the idea of *tzniut* is supported or not supported by today's lifestyle?**
- **How has the concept of what acceptable clothing is changed over time – would your grandparents dress the way you dress?**
- **Would your parents have dressed that way when they were your age?**

What are the standards for how we dress and who sets them?

Think of some different locations such as school, synagogue, USY trips, or work. Discuss what appropriate dress is for each setting. Try to identify the purpose for conducting the activity or session at each locale and then reexamine whether or not the clothing pattern that you suggested originally is consistent with the goal and purpose of the activity.

Think about how some young people come dressed for synagogue services. Do you think it makes sense for USY to have a policy in place then? **Should *synagogues* have a dress policy that reflects the value of Tzniut? Where do you draw the line?** Should all Conservative synagogues establish a unified dress code, or is part of the issue what individual congregations find appropriate and honorable?

USY has a dress policy that begins with the following statement:

> Tzniut (modesty) is a long-standing Jewish value. As a people who see ourselves as reflecting the image of God, our Jewish community believes we should act accordingly; thus, some things are not appropriate, for they do not reflect our Jewish values. How we dress is a basic example of these values.
>
> "The privacy which Judaism requires of sex (in Hebrew, *tzniut*, modesty) affects our clothing, or speech, and our public activities. We may dress in accord with the styles of the times, but never should our apparel accentuate the sexually arousing parts of our bodies. Thus sexually suggestive or revealing clothes for either men or women are not in keeping with Jewish law or sensibilities." (Rabbinical Assembly, Rabbinic Letter on Intimate Relations).

Why do you think a policy about a dress code would begin with a statement about Tzniut and modesty?

This policy represents the minimum expectations for modest and appropriate dress at USY events. It is divided into two sections, one for all USY activities and the other for Shabbat.

We have included only the section for all general USY activities:

BASIC USY STANDARDS OF DRESS

Clothing on which any profanity or inappropriate language, pictures or symbols are written, printed or depicted is not permitted.

No visible underwear is permitted for both males and females.

During Tefillah, inappropriately short skirts or shorts, or tight garments, are not permitted; shoulders must be covered for both males and females.

Tank tops, 2-piece bathing suits (except where midriff is covered), bare midriff styles, halter-tops, leggings, or see-through blouses are not permitted.

- *How does Tzniut convey self respect?*
- *Does a really short skirt or a t-shirt with inappropriate language mean the wearer doesn't respect him/herself?*
- *How does appropriate appearance convey self respect, self esteem and the Jewish concept of B'tzelem Elohim?*

When you dress appropriately, you convey the message that you appreciate yourself and regard yourself with dignity and respect—your inside feelings match your outside appearance.

If you were to invent an item or style of clothing which was both modern and consistent with Jewish tradition, that would identify an individual as Jewish, what would you design? How would you get people to adopt it as a pattern of dress?

Wearing modest clothing can also remind us to behave appropriately.

לז וַיֹּאמֶר יְהוָה, אֶל-מֹשֶׁה לֵּאמֹר.

37 And the Lord spoke unto Moses, saying:

לח דַּבֵּר אֶל-בְּנֵי יִשְׂרָאֵל, וְאָמַרְתָּ אֲלֵהֶם, וְעָשׂוּ לָהֶם צִיצִת עַל-כַּנְפֵי בִגְדֵיהֶם, לְדֹרֹתָם; וְנָתְנוּ עַל-צִיצִת הַכָּנָף, פְּתִיל תְּכֵלֶת.

38 Speak unto the children of Israel, and instruct them that they make them throughout their generations fringes in the corners of their garments, and that they put with the fringe of each corner a thread of blue.

לט וְהָיָה לָכֶם, לְצִיצִת, וּרְאִיתֶם אֹתוֹ וּזְכַרְתֶּם אֶת-כָּל-מִצְוֹת יְהוָה, וַעֲשִׂיתֶם אֹתָם; וְלֹא-תָתוּרוּ אַחֲרֵי לְבַבְכֶם, וְאַחֲרֵי עֵינֵיכֶם, אֲשֶׁר-אַתֶּם זֹנִים, אַחֲרֵיהֶם.

39 And it shall be unto you for a fringe, that you may look upon it, and remember all the commandments of the Lord, and do them; and that you go not about after your own heart and your own eyes, after which you use to go astray;

(Bamidbar 15:37-39)

The tzitzit are such a special garment that it is not hard to imagine that they can act as a reminder to act properly. *How can our own dress (even for those of us who do not wear tzitzit) act as a brake on our improper urges?*

Read and discuss this story from the Talmud (Menakhot 44a):

> R. Nathan said, There is not a single precept in the Torah, even the lightest, whose reward is not enjoyed in this world; and as to its reward in the future world I know not how great it is. Go and learn this from the precept of tzitzit. Once a man, who was very scrupulous about the precept of tzitzit, heard of a certain harlot in one of the towns by the sea who accepted four hundred gold [denars] for her hire. He sent her four hundred gold [denars] and appointed a day with her. When the day arrived he came and waited at her door, and her maid came and told her, 'That man who sent you four hundred gold [denars] is here and waiting at the door'; to which she replied 'Let him come in'. When he came in she prepared for him seven beds, six of silver and one of gold; and between one bed and the other there were steps of silver, but the last were of gold. She then went up to the top bed and lay down upon it naked. He too went up after her in his desire to sit naked with her, when all of a sudden the four fringes [of his garment] struck him across the face; whereupon he slipped off and sat upon the ground. She also slipped off and sat upon the ground and said, 'By the Roman Capitol, I will not leave you alone until you tell me what blemish you saw in me. 'By the Temple', he replied, 'never have I seen a woman as beautiful as you are; but there is one precept which the Lord our God has commanded us, it is called tzitzit, and with regard to it the expression 'I am the Lord your God' is twice written, signifying, I am He who will exact punishment in the future, and I am He who will give reward in the future. Now [the tzitzit] appeared to me as four witnesses [testifying against me]'. She said, 'I will not leave you until you tell me your name, the name of your town, the name of your teacher, the name of your school in which you study the Torah'. He wrote all this down and handed it to her. Thereupon she arose and divided her estate into three parts; one third for the government, one third to be distributed among the poor, and one third she took with her in her hand; the bed clothes, however, she retained. She then came to the Beth Hamidrash of R. Hiyya, and said to him, 'Master, give instructions about me that they make me a proselyte'. 'My daughter', he replied; 'perhaps you have set your eyes on one of the disciples?' She thereupon took out the script and handed it to him. 'Go', said he 'and enjoy your acquisition'. Those very bed-clothes which she had spread for him for an illicit purpose she now spread out for him lawfully.

Apply the question from above to this story—**How can our own dress (even for those of us who do not wear tzitzit) act as a brake on our improper urges?**

Do you find your behavior changes when you are dressed in nicer clothing —are you more likely to act respectfully when wearing a suit than you are when wearing a swimsuit or backward baseball hat?

We wear Tallit to pray but some people choose to wear Tallit Katan (a type of undergarment vest with tzitzit on the ends) every day, all day. Does this story help you understand why people do that? Would having a constant reminder help you make better choices in terms of behavior? Would wearing tzitzit help remind you to perform more mitzvot?

Activity: Would You Rather...

Two options of "would you rather" are presented below. Place your answers on the line where you think you fit. You may not be clear if you want "A" or "B"— in that case, put your answer where you think it should fall on the line.

Would you rather have (A) big muscles or (B) ideal facial features?

A _____ B

Would you rather have a best friend who is (A) "cool" and good looking but constantly disappoints you or (B) someone who's loyal and dedicated to you but kind of "geeky" in nature and appearance?

A _____ B

Would you rather be (A) "Hollywood beautiful" or (B) get into the dream college of your choice?

A _____ B

Would you rather (A) have a beautiful face or (B) be considered one of the funniest people around?

A _____ B

Would you rather (A) be respected at your job for skill and intellect or (B) have a job where you need to "look perfect" to succeed but it's a fun job and pays really well?

A _____ B

Would you rather (A) have a less than perfect body but be in great shape or (B) have a "perfect body" but not be able to climb stairs easily?

A _____ B

At your 10 year High School, reunion, would you want people to be in awe of (A) how good you look or at (B) what you've accomplished?

A _____ B

What did you learn from this exercise? Do you feel that you have the right priorities according to your choices? Is your outside more important to you than your inside? How can you behave to reflect what matters most to you?

God and My Bod: a Checklist

You are holy. What choices do you make that reflect this? The choices you make determine how others will perceive you and how you perceive yourself.

Activity: Inside vs. Outside

On my Body (outer)
- [ ] I think about how I dress – I choose clothes that respect myself as a holy being.
- [ ] My outside choices match my inside feelings
- [ ] What I present today on the outside, is what I want people to think of me
- [ ] What I'm wearing is right for me

In my Body (inner)
- [ ] I choose healthy food to eat to give me energy and strength
- [ ] I exercise
- [ ] I choose to use my time wisely
- [ ] I sleep enough so that I can fully participate in the day
- [ ] I compliment myself or gave myself credit for an accomplishment
- [ ] I laugh and smile
- [ ] I am good to a friend
- [ ] I ask for help from a friend
- [ ] I challenge myself to think today
- [ ] I try to see the positive side of a situation
- [ ] I problem solve
- [ ] I have something to look forward to
- [ ] I will speak with kindness and respect, to my parents, siblings, friends and teachers
- [ ] I will hold a door open, say hello to a stranger, make someone feel welcome

We've focused on the inside and outside of what comprises a complete "you," and learned that each of us is unique, made in the image of God and holy in the way we care for ourselves with respect and dignity as a creation of God. How can we be holy in terms of interacting with others?

Chapter Six
Being A mensch

What does it mean to be a mensch?
Acting according to the laws of derech eretz can also be called *"Menschlechkeit"* or being a mensch. Literally, mensch means "man" but in today's more egalitarian world, we use it to mean "being a good person" or behaving with Derech Eretz.

What does it take to "be a mensch?"

בְּמָקוֹם שֶׁאֵין אֲנָשִׁים, הִשְׁתַּדֵּל לִהְיוֹת אִישׁ

Where there are no worthy persons, strive to be a worthy person.

(Pirkei Avot 2:6)

Scenario One:
You're on the basketball team and in the locker room, a bunch of guys are bothering one of the other team members. They're teasing him about random things he can't help—his glasses, his height, even the color of his hair (red!). It's not affecting you at all so you don't bother interrupting them to defend him.

Should you say something? If so, what would you say? If not, why would you stay quiet?

"A person who loves a friend cannot stand by and watch that friend be beaten or insulted. The person would come to the friend's aid" – Rabbi Moshe Chaim Luzzato, Mesilat Yesharim 19:17

Make yourself a mensch and speak up. If you know it's not right, why wouldn't you say something? If it's not about you though, why should you? By standing up for this person you are showing you respect him. You are giving him a level of dignity the others are trying to destroy.

The Meaning of Mensch
- ***What is a mensch?***
- ***What qualities does a mensch exhibit?***
- ***What are the barriers to menschlechkeit for males particularly? Is it not macho to be a mensch?***
- ***Can a girl be a mensch? What types of things could a girl to do be a mensch?***
- ***Do you sometimes fear that it isn't cool to stand up for someone being teased or to perform acts of kindness? What do you think holds you back from mensch-like behavior?***
- ***What makes a "man?" Who do teenage males look to as role models?***

Males: Who do you look up to?

Thinking about men I see in film, TV or on the news, the most "manly man" I see is _____.

Thinking about "real people" in my life, the most "manly man" I know is _____ because _____.

I want to look like _____ from film or TV.

I want to be like _____ because _____

There are many different places we can turn to find positive (and not so positive) role models. As Jews, we can always turn to our biblical ancestors as role models for both males and females. Who in our biblical and rabbinic ancestry can we rely on as a good example of what it means to be a man beyond muscles—a mensch?

Muscle Man

Samson, like Superman, was mighty and muscular but relied on his hair, the secret source of his strength. His strength eventually is what kills him. Being a mensch means more than muscles.

יז וַיַּגֶּד-לָהּ אֶת-כָּל-לִבּוֹ, וַיֹּאמֶר לָהּ מוֹרָה לֹא-עָלָה עַל-רֹאשִׁי—כִּי-נְזִיר אֱלֹהִים אֲנִי, מִבֶּטֶן אִמִּי; אִם-גֻּלַּחְתִּי וְסָר מִמֶּנִּי כֹחִי, וְחָלִיתִי וְהָיִיתִי כְּכָל-הָאָדָם.

17 And he told her all his heart, and said to her: 'There has not come a razor upon my head; for I have been a Nazirite unto God from my mother's womb; if I be shaven, then my strength will go from me, and I shall become weak, and be like any other man.'

(Shoftim 16:17)

Samson loses his power:

כא וַיֹּאחֲזוּהוּ פְלִשְׁתִּים, וַיְנַקְּרוּ אֶת-עֵינָיו; וַיּוֹרִידוּ אוֹתוֹ עַזָּתָה, וַיַּאַסְרוּהוּ בַּנְחֻשְׁתַּיִם, וַיְהִי טוֹחֵן, בְּבֵית האסירים (הָאֲסוּרִים).

21 And the Philistines laid hold on him, and put out his eyes; and they brought him down to Gaza, and bound him with fetters of brass; and he did grind in the prison-house.

(Shoftim 16:21)

Samson's strength kills him:

ל וַיֹּאמֶר שִׁמְשׁוֹן, תָּמוֹת נַפְשִׁי עִם-פְּלִשְׁתִּים, וַיֵּט בְּכֹחַ, וַיִּפֹּל הַבַּיִת עַל-הַסְּרָנִים וְעַל-כָּל-הָעָם אֲשֶׁר-בּוֹ; וַיִּהְיוּ הַמֵּתִים, אֲשֶׁר הֵמִית בְּמוֹתוֹ, רַבִּים, מֵאֲשֶׁר הֵמִית בְּחַיָּיו.

30 And Samson said: 'Let me die with the Philistines.' And he bent with all his might; and the house fell upon the lords, and upon all the people that were therein. So the dead that he slew at his death were more than they that he slew in his life.

(Shoftim 16:30)

Muscles will not make you a better person (unless you use them to help others such as by carrying groceries or helping mom or dad move furniture). Your choices, values and virtues make you a mensch or a man.

What characteristics do you think are "menschly," true examples of masculinity or "manliness?"

Take a look at the following texts. Then, complete the activity that follows.

TEXT ONE: Supporting a wife—Elkanah, the husband of Hannah

Hannah is depressed because she is unable to conceive a child. Elkanah shows her his love and support.

ה וּלְחַנָּה, יִתֵּן מָנָה אַחַת אַפָּיִם : כִּי אֶת-חַנָּה אָהֵב, וַיהוָה סָגַר רַחְמָהּ.

5 but unto Hannah he gave a double portion; for he loved Hannah, but the God had shut up her womb.

(I Shmuel 1:5)

Elkanah tries to reassure his wife and tries to support her despite her sadness:

ח וַיֹּאמֶר לָהּ אֶלְקָנָה אִישָׁהּ, חַנָּה לָמֶה תִבְכִּי וְלָמֶה לֹא תֹאכְלִי, וְלָמֶה, יֵרַע לְבָבֵךְ : הֲלוֹא אָנֹכִי טוֹב לָךְ, מֵעֲשָׂרָה בָּנִים.

8 And Elkanah her husband said unto her: 'Hannah, why do you weep? and why have you not eaten? and why is your heart grieved? am I not better to you than ten sons?'

(I Shmuel 1:8)

TEXT TWO: Supporting a sister—Recall the Dinah narrative.

Her brothers seek revenge on her behalf, as protective siblings.

ז וּבְנֵי יַעֲקֹב בָּאוּ מִן-הַשָּׂדֶה, כְּשָׁמְעָם, וַיִּתְעַצְּבוּ הָאֲנָשִׁים, וַיִּחַר לָהֶם מְאֹד : כִּי-נְבָלָה עָשָׂה בְיִשְׂרָאֵל, לִשְׁכַּב אֶת-בַּת-יַעֲקֹב, וְכֵן, לֹא יֵעָשֶׂה.

7 And the sons of Jacob came in from the field when they heard it; and the men were grieved, and they were very wroth, because he had wrought a vile deed in Israel in lying with Jacob's daughter; which thing ought not to be done.

כז בְּנֵי יַעֲקֹב, בָּאוּ עַל-הַחֲלָלִים, וַיָּבֹזּוּ, הָעִיר—אֲשֶׁר טִמְּאוּ, אֲחוֹתָם.

27 The sons of Jacob came upon the slain, and spoiled the city, because they [the people of the city of Hamor] had defiled their sister.

(Bereishit 34:7, 27)

Was revenge a "manly" thing to do? How would you have handled the situation if someone had brutally hurt your sister?

TEXT THREE: Kindness to Strangers—Abraham hosts the Angels

Abraham does all he can to ensure the comfort of his guests (note for pasuk/verse 8 that laws of Kashrut were not yet commanded!)

ב וַיִּשָּׂא עֵינָיו, וַיַּרְא, וְהִנֵּה שְׁלֹשָׁה אֲנָשִׁים, נִצָּבִים עָלָיו ; וַיַּרְא, וַיָּרָץ לִקְרָאתָם מִפֶּתַח הָאֹהֶל, וַיִּשְׁתַּחוּ, אָרְצָה.

2 and he lifted up his eyes and looked, and three men stood over against him; and when he saw them, he ran to meet them from the tent door, and bowed down to the earth,

ה וְאֶקְחָה פַת-לֶחֶם וְסַעֲדוּ לִבְּכֶם, אַחַר תַּעֲבֹרוּ—כִּי-עַל-כֵּן עֲבַרְתֶּם, עַל-עַבְדְּכֶם ; וַיֹּאמְרוּ, כֵּן תַּעֲשֶׂה כַּאֲשֶׁר דִּבַּרְתָּ.

5 And I will fetch a morsel of bread, and stay your heart; after that you shall pass on; forasmuch as you are come to your servant.' And they said: 'So do, as you have said.'

ח וַיִּקַּח חֶמְאָה וְחָלָב, וּבֶן-הַבָּקָר אֲשֶׁר עָשָׂה, וַיִּתֵּן, לִפְנֵיהֶם ; וְהוּא-עֹמֵד עֲלֵיהֶם תַּחַת הָעֵץ, וַיֹּאכֵלוּ.

8 And he took curd, and milk, and the calf which he had dressed, and set it before them; and he stood by them under the tree, and they ate.

(Bereishit 18:2, 5, 8)

TEXT FOUR: Ruling with Compassion and Fairness—King Solomon:
Two woman give birth around the same time. One child dies. The mother of the dead child claims the other mother stole her baby. They are brought before King Solomon for his famous judgment:

כד וַיֹּאמֶר הַמֶּלֶךְ, קְחוּ לִי-חָרֶב; וַיָּבִאוּ הַחֶרֶב, לִפְנֵי הַמֶּלֶךְ.

24 And the king said: 'Fetch me a sword.' And they brought a sword before the king.

כה וַיֹּאמֶר הַמֶּלֶךְ, גִּזְרוּ אֶת-הַיֶּלֶד הַחַי לִשְׁנָיִם; וּתְנוּ אֶת-הַחֲצִי לְאַחַת, וְאֶת-הַחֲצִי לְאֶחָת.

25 And the king said: 'Divide the living child in two, and give half to the one, and half to the other.'

כו וַתֹּאמֶר הָאִשָּׁה אֲשֶׁר-בְּנָהּ הַחַי אֶל-הַמֶּלֶךְ, כִּי-נִכְמְרוּ רַחֲמֶיהָ עַל-בְּנָהּ, וַתֹּאמֶר בִּי אֲדֹנִי תְּנוּ-לָהּ אֶת-הַיָּלוּד הַחַי, וְהָמֵת אַל-תְּמִיתֻהוּ; וְזֹאת אֹמֶרֶת, גַּם-לִי גַם-לָךְ לֹא יִהְיֶה—גְּזֹרוּ.

26 Then spoke the woman who was the mother of the living child to the king, for her heart yearned upon her son, and she said: 'Oh, my lord, give her the living child, and don't slay it.' But the other said: 'It shall be neither mine nor hers; divide it.'

כז וַיַּעַן הַמֶּלֶךְ וַיֹּאמֶר, תְּנוּ-לָהּ אֶת-הַיָּלוּד הַחַי, וְהָמֵת, לֹא תְמִיתֻהוּ: הִיא, אִמּוֹ.

27 Then the king answered and said: 'Give her the living child, and don't slay it: she is the mother.'

(I Melachim 3:24-27)

TEXT FIVE: Bosom Buddies—Loving your friends—Recall David and Jonathan:

יז וַיּוֹסֶף יְהוֹנָתָן לְהַשְׁבִּיעַ אֶת-דָּוִד, בְּאַהֲבָתוֹ אֹתוֹ: כִּי-אַהֲבַת נַפְשׁוֹ, אֲהֵבוֹ.

17 And Jonathan caused David to swear again, for the love that he had to him; for he loved him as he loved his own soul.

(I Shmu'el 20:17)

Most men may not consider it "manly" to show love, affection or appreciation for a male friend. Being there for your friends and showing support toward a male friend is not only acceptable, but "menschly." Many teen males are comfortable hugging or jumping on their buddies with affection, some others may consider this something "men just don't do." Some father and son duos only shake hands. It is acceptable and appropriate to love and respect a best friend.

TEXT SIX: Kindness—Boaz in the Book of Ruth- A "man of valor"
Following the death of her husband, Ruth follows her mother in law, Naomi to Moab. Boaz, a man described as "a man of valor" (אִישׁ גִּבּוֹר) reaches out to her and shows her the kindness and compassion that she had exhibited to Naomi.

ח וַיֹּאמֶר בֹּעַז אֶל-רוּת הֲלוֹא שָׁמַעַתְּ בִּתִּי, אַל-תֵּלְכִי לִלְקֹט בְּשָׂדֶה אַחֵר, וְגַם לֹא תַעֲבוּרִי, מִזֶּה; וְכֹה תִדְבָּקִין, עִם-נַעֲרֹתָי.

8 Then said Boaz to Ruth: "I don't hear you, my daughter? Don't glean in another field, neither pass from hence, but stay here with my maidens.

ט עֵינַיִךְ בַּשָּׂדֶה אֲשֶׁר-יִקְצֹרוּן, וְהָלַכְתְּ אַחֲרֵיהֶן—הֲלוֹא צִוִּיתִי אֶת-הַנְּעָרִים, לְבִלְתִּי נָגְעֵךְ; וְצָמִת, וְהָלַכְתְּ אֶל-הַכֵּלִים, וְשָׁתִית, מֵאֲשֶׁר יִשְׁאֲבוּן הַנְּעָרִים.

9 Let your eyes be on the field that they do reap, and you go after them; have I not charged the young men that they shall not touch you? and when you are thirsty, go to the vessels, and drink of that which the young men have drawn.'

י וַתִּפֹּל, עַל-פָּנֶיהָ, וַתִּשְׁתַּחוּ, אָרְצָה ; וַתֹּאמֶר אֵלָיו, מַדּוּעַ מָצָאתִי חֵן בְּעֵינֶיךָ לְהַכִּירֵנִי— וְאָנֹכִי, נָכְרִיָּה.

10 Then she fell on her face, and bowed down to the ground, and said unto him: 'Why have I found favor in thy sight, that you should take care of me, seeing I am a foreigner?'

יא וַיַּעַן בֹּעַז, וַיֹּאמֶר לָהּ—הֻגֵּד הֻגַּד לִי כֹּל אֲשֶׁר-עָשִׂית אֶת-חֲמוֹתֵךְ, אַחֲרֵי מוֹת אִישֵׁךְ ; וַתַּעַזְבִי אָבִיךְ וְאִמֵּךְ, וְאֶרֶץ מוֹלַדְתֵּךְ, וַתֵּלְכִי, אֶל-עַם אֲשֶׁר לֹא-יָדַעַתְּ תְּמוֹל שִׁלְשׁוֹם.

11 And Boaz answered and said unto her: 'It has fully been told me, all that thou have done for your mother-in-law since the death of your husband; and how you have left your father and your mother, and the land of your nativity, and have come to a people that you did not know.

יד וַיֹּאמֶר לָהּ בֹעַז לְעֵת הָאֹכֶל, גֹּשִׁי הֲלֹם וְאָכַלְתְּ מִן-הַלֶּחֶם, וְטָבַלְתְּ פִּתֵּךְ, בַּחֹמֶץ ; וַתֵּשֶׁב, מִצַּד הַקֹּצְרִים, וַיִּצְבָּט-לָהּ קָלִי, וַתֹּאכַל וַתִּשְׂבַּע וַתֹּתַר.

14 And Boaz said to her at meal-time: 'Come here, and eat of the bread, and dip your morsel in the vinegar.' And she sat beside the reapers; and they reached her parched corn, and she did eat and was satisfied, and left from there.

טו וַתָּקָם, לְלַקֵּט ; וַיְצַו בֹּעַז אֶת-נְעָרָיו לֵאמֹר, גַּם בֵּין הָעֳמָרִים תְּלַקֵּט—וְלֹא תַכְלִימוּהָ.

15 And when she rose up to glean, Boaz commanded his young men, saying: 'Let her glean even among the sheaves, and don't shame her.

(Megillat Ruth 2:8, 9-11, 14-15)

Activity: More than Muscles

As we can see from these examples, being a man goes beyond muscles. Being "manly" means exhibiting "menschly" behavior. What are some examples of "menschly" behavior?

Using the examples from the texts in this chapter, how can you demonstrate mensch like behavior toward your:

Text 1: significant other/eventual spouse:

Text 2: sister

Text 3: guests

Text 4: group that you lead

Text 5: male friend

Text 6: parental figure

Activity: Modern Menschen

Above, we've outlined examples of biblical menschen or manly men. Can you think of examples from modern Jewish history of men who exhibited fine examples of mensch-like behavior or possessed mensch-like characteristics? Who would receive the "Honorable Menschen" award?

Example:
Person: Abraham Joshua Heschel
Characteristic/accomplishment: Was not only a brilliant Jewish scholar but was committed to social justice and equality

Person:
Characteristic/accomplishment:

Person:
Characteristic/accomplishment:

Person:
Characteristic/accomplishment:

Person:
Characteristic/accomplishment:

Chapter Seven
The Power of Words

Words are powerful, and can be destructive to relationships. Although we spend a lot of time gossiping about each other and spreading rumors, talking about other people is prohibited in Judaism unless the information is absolutely necessary. We are required to think favorably of other people, even when we hear rumors that might put them in a bad light. Technology enables rumors to be spread very quickly and we must be extremely careful before sending any messages that might be embarrassing to another person. Good communication however is a critical component of a healthy relationship.

The power of words was described centuries ago in the Tanach:
Words can be beautiful flowers or poisonous weeds, capable of building or destroying a personal relationship.

כא מָוֶת וְחַיִּים, בְּיַד-לָשׁוֹן ; וְאֹהֲבֶיהָ, יֹאכַל פִּרְיָהּ.

21 Death and life are in the power of the tongue; and they that indulge it shall eat the fruit thereof.

(Mishlei 18:21)

Words are so commonplace that we often do not stop to think about them and the way in which they ought to be used. Taking them for granted, we often value their power less than we should.

Communication and Relationships
Focus on "I," not "You"

Why is communication an important part of friendships and relationships? **What are some 'good' and 'bad' ways to communicate?**
A good way to communicate is _____.
A bad way to communicate is _____.
Important characteristics of healthy communication are:

Talking through problems and disagreements isn't easy, but there are some ways to help make sure you are positive and constructive in finding solutions and coming to agreements.

One way is by making sure you focus on your opinions and feelings, and try not to place blame. Here's an example:

"You" statement: "You always pick fights with me."
"I" statement: "It makes me upset that we keep fighting."

What is the difference between these two statements? What are the different kinds of responses that these statements would evoke? (Think about the responses that are both verbal and emotional.)

The first statement focuses on the other person in this conversation, and the blaming tone might cause the argument to escalate. The second statement focuses on the person speaking, and his or her own feelings. It does not blame either party.

Find a friend and practice a conversation that you might have based on one of the scenarios below. First, have the conversation using "you" statements. Then, try it with "I" statements. Respond honestly, the way you think you would in a real conversation.

Scenario 1

You and a friend have made plans to go out a few times, but each time, your friend calls and cancels at the last minute. This weekend the two of you have plans to meet for dinner at the new vegan restaurant and then hang out. Just as you get there, your friend calls you and says she accidentally 'double booked' and can't meet you.

How did your "you" statement conversation go? Your "I" statement conversation?
What was the difference? Did each conversation have a different outcome?

Arguments and disagreements are part of almost any relationship; the sign of a healthy relationship is being able to talk about them and find solutions or resolutions that you are both comfortable with.

It is also very important that you feel you are able to communicate your thoughts, opinions and feelings to your friend or significant other. Of course, he or she should feel the same way.

Activity—Role Play

Write a scenario in which two people are having a disagreement. Then, role play using "you" and "I" statements.

Scenario: _____

_____

_____

_____.

Scenario 2

You were recently introduced to your friend's girlfriend. Your friend is very excited and after she leaves, asks you what you think. You have heard a few rumors about the girlfriend and are not sure whether or not to share them.

What do you do?

Terms to Know

Shmirat Halashon (guarding your tongue, watching your words, thinking before you speak)
Lashon Hara (evil speech)
Rechilut (talebearing, gossip)
Motzi Shem Ra- a slanderer (i.e. calling someone a name, giving him/her a bad name)

It often seems that a lot of our time is spent talking about other people's personal lives. It may seem perfectly acceptable to do this as the line between public and private has been so blurred by the media's attention to the salacious details of famous people and popular television shows which are based primarily on talking about other people (think for example about the shows *Gossip Girl* and *The Housewives*). The use of technology in spreading rumors and gossip has sped up the already fast pace by which information – both true and untrue, kind and unkind, private and public, is shared. It may be perfectly acceptable in today's world, but according to Jewish Law, talking about other people is not permitted except under very strict guidelines.

Spreading rumors and gossiping are often the source of untold damage and misery and both are forbidden by Jewish law. The commandment of *shmirat ha'lashon* means literally "to watch our tongue." This is an incredibly difficult commandment to keep and the rabbis recognized that. The basic premise of *shmirat ha'lashon* is that we should not talk about other people, unless there is a particular reason why it is important to share information about someone – even when what we are saying is true.

We are taught to guard against all types of forbidden speech. Truth is no defense to speaking badly about someone —Lashon hara are derogatory but true statements about someone else, told when there was no need for the information to be shared.

- *What could possibly be the problem with sharing true information about someone?*
- *How would you determine if someone needed to know the information?*
- *How do you determine if a statement about someone is true or not?*
- *What would you talk about if you didn't talk about other people?*
- *Think back on some conversations you've had recently with your friends. What did you talk about? How much of the time was spent talking about other friends or kids you know?*

לשון תליתאי קטיל תליתאי, הורג Gossip kills three people: the speaker, the listener
למספרו ולמקבלו ולאומרו and the person being discussed.
(Babylonian Talmud, Arachin, 15b)

How does gossip hurt each of the three parties involved?

The speaker is hurt by _____.

The listener is hurt by _____.

The person being spoken about is hurt by _____.

Here are some types of *lashon hara*. Can you think of examples of each? Feel free to add your own categories as well.

Derogatory statements:
Damaging someone's reputation:
Insults:
Highlighting someone's faults:

Rechilut—Gossip

Rechilut is a type of *lashon hara* and is any communication that causes animosity between people. In particular, we are guilty of *rechilut* when we tell the person being talked about what was said about him or her. This is prohibited because of the harm it can cause to a relationship.

Another type of *lashon hara* is *motzi shem ra* – spreading a bad name or slandering a person – in these cases, the person is spreading false statements about someone else – clearly a way to cause acrimony and harm.

Why do you think this is particularly harmful?

Think about times when someone told you what someone else said about you.
- *How did you react?*
- *How did it affect your friendship or relationship with the gossiper?*
- *How did it affect your friendship or relationship with the person who talked about you initially?*

Now think about times when you told someone what someone else said about her or him.
What was your motive?
Do you think your motive justified your action?

ח דִּבְרֵי נִרְגָּן, כְּמִתְלַהֲמִים; וְהֵם, יָרְדוּ חַדְרֵי-בָטֶן.

8 The words of a talebearer are as wounds, and they go down into the innermost parts of the belly.

(Mishlei 18:8)

טז לֹא-תֵלֵךְ רָכִיל בְּעַמֶּיךָ, לֹא תַעֲמֹד עַל-דַּם רֵעֶךָ: אֲנִי, יְהוָה.

16 You shall not go up and down as a talebearer among your people; neither shall you stand idly by the blood of your neighbor: I am the Lord.

(Vayikra 19:16)

Why does the second half of this statement follow the first half? How do they connect to each other? Try putting this verse into your own words to help explain it.

When words can be hurtful _____

When words can help _____

ז מִדְּבַר-שֶׁקֶר, תִּרְחָק; וְנָקִי וְצַדִּיק אַל-תַּהֲרֹג, כִּי לֹא-אַצְדִּיק רָשָׁע.

7 Distance yourself from false words; and the innocent and righteous slay thou not; for I will not justify the wicked.

(Shmot 23:7)

What does this mean? Why is it important?

Gossip is addictive. It is human nature to gossip but staying clear of gossip is the right thing to do.
What strategies can you employ to "distance yourself from false words?"

Think back to our discussion about distancing oneself from people with bad intentions. This is the same principle. The people around us can impact how we think and act, and if we make sure we surround ourselves with people who speak appropriately and truthfully, we will help ensure that we do the same.

This choice of language also encompasses the idea of distancing oneself not only from people who speak gossip and rumors, but also from gossip and rumors in general—even if you hear *lashon hara*, it does not mean you have to accept or believe it. You can push those false words away, as well as the people who speak them.

In the earlier chapter about friendship we discussed the Mishna from Pirkei Avot (1:6) that listed three important things that enrich our lives: finding a mentor, finding a friend, and *dan l'chaf zechut*, judging every person favorably and giving him or her the benefit of the doubt.

How does the principle of judging another person favorably, dan l'kaf zechut, apply when it comes to gossip and rumors?

According to the Rambam, a person must go out of his way to think of a reason that would excuse a seemingly sinful act, even if the only reason he can come up with seems illogical or impossible.

Scenario 3: Notes

While walking down the hall in school, you see Sarah whispering with Josh, Jennifer's boyfriend of two years. During class, you see Sarah and Josh passing notes back and forth. During lunch, another friend, Michelle, tells you she thinks Josh and Sarah have been hanging out a lot recently; she saw them together at the mall this weekend, and they both ducked away when Michelle saw them. Michelle tells you she thinks Josh is cheating on Jennifer with Sarah.

If you were going to *dan l'chaf zechut*, what would you do?
Tell someone else you think Josh is cheating on Jennifer with Sarah
Tell someone that Josh and Sarah were passing notes in class
Tell Michelle there isn't any evidence of cheating, and that rumors can really hurt

The real story: Josh asked Sarah to help him plan a surprise party for Jennifer, whose birthday is coming up next week.

Why is it hard to *dan l'chaf zechut*, judge others favorably, all the time?

Think of a rumor you have heard recently. *Did you dan l'chaf zechut?*
   If yes, how?
   If not, how could you have?

Ru·mor [roo – mer] *noun*
A story or statement in general circulation without confirmation or certainty as to facts
Gossip or hearsay

- *How do rumors start?*
- *How are rumors spread?*
- *How can rumors impact the object of the rumor?*
- *Are both speakers and listeners at fault for the spread of rumors?*
- *How do rumors end? Is there a way to get rid of the rumor, or reverse the damage done?*

Think about a rumor someone spread about you.

- *How did that rumor make you feel?*
- *Did the rumor impact the way others interact with you? Why or why not?*
- *Did the rumor affect your reputation or standing in your social circle? Why or why not?*
- *How did you react to the rumor?*

Activity: I heard a Rumor

Think about all of the feelings and emotions that rumor evoked for you. In the space below, use magazine cut-outs of pictures, words or letters, to create a collage that represents those feelings and emotions.

Gossip and rumors feel like: _____.

Gossip on Television: Gossip Girl Exposed

The CW network hit, *Gossip Girl,* thrives off of the human desire to know everything about everyone. The "Gossip Girl" of the show is a secret blogger who dishes about the goings-on of Upper East Side teens. The intimate details of these privileged teen lives become everyone's business. To teens who are used to having everything, they must live their lives without two basic human needs—privacy and trust.

Think back to our discussion on what makes a good friend? What does Gossip Girl *teach us about trust and loyalty between friends?*

For people who seem to "have it all," why do they also need to "know it all?" *What happens with the information they learn about each other? Why do you think this blogger needs to share the intimate details of the lives of those around her with the world? Why would anyone care to know everything about everyone?*

Taking it further: Apply this to today's reality television shows where the camera enters the private lives of families. These shows are smash hits, elevating ordinary people into super-stars. We live in a culture of "open windows" where our lives are so easily exposed and complete strangers know more about us than our own parents might. *What happens when the lives of others become dinner table conversation of the average family? Do you think reality TV families deserve to suffer the consequences of public opinion and gossip because they chose to share their lives on national television?*

What are the consequences of details of your life being shared with the world? What do we learn from shows that trivialize or ignore the effects of gossip, perpetuating the habit of talking about others and spreading information that is not ours to share?

What are the dangers of these types of shows to our culture? What values are at stake when these shows become popular among the young generation?

The Power of the Tongue

כא מָוֶת וְחַיִּים, בְּיַד-לָשׁוֹן; וְאֹהֲבֶיהָ, יֹאכַל פִּרְיָהּ.

21 Death and life are in the power of the tongue. Those who use it well will eat its fruit.

(Mishlei 18:21)

יב דִּבְרֵי פִי-חָכָם, חֵן; וְשִׂפְתוֹת כְּסִיל, תְּבַלְּעֶנּוּ.

12 A wise man's words bring him favor; a fool's lips are his undoing.

(Kohelet 10:12)

What do we learn from these texts about the power of our words?
Is something that is powerful easy or hard to control?

The laws about honesty, authenticity and integrity of speech are probably as extensive as the Jewish dietary laws of kashrut. This ought not come as a surprise, since speech is the primary medium of human interaction. Speech is not the whole of human ethics, but a very large part of it. We will soon see that a Jew is forbidden to insult, shame, embarrass, defame, slander, curse, or swear falsely.

The Talmudic rabbis were also deeply aware of the power of speech and communication. The misuse of words includes the use of profanity and foul language as well as tale bearing and gossiping about a person. Wanting to make the people aware of it as well, they wrote many stories and were quoted many times concerning their attitude on the use of language

Maimonides, the great medieval philosopher, defined slander of the tongue as speaking disparagingly about anyone (even though what is spoken may be the truth!). The sages equated the use of the evil tongue with idolatry, incest and even murder. It is doubtful whether the rabbis meant this equation to be taken literally. It was, however, their way of demonstrating their hope that people would avoid committing the crime of slander and gossip by equating them with three of the gravest sins.

It is noteworthy that of all transgressions, evil talk is perhaps the one that is easiest to commit, but its effects can be potent enough to destroy a person's reputation.

Rabban Shimon ben Gamliel said to Tavi, his servant: "Go to the market and buy me something good." Tavi went to the market and bought tongue. The Rav then sent Tavi to buy something bad. Tavi came back with tongue. "What is going on here?" asked Rabban Shimon. "I ask you to buy something good and you buy tongue. I ask you to buy something bad and you buy tongue." Tavi replied, "There are good and bad tongues. When a tongue speaks properly, there is nothing better than it. And when a tongue does not speak nicely, there is nothing worse than it"…

… During a festive meal that Rebbe Yehuda HaNassi made for his students, he served both soft, perfectly cooked tongues and hard, overcooked tongues. The students selected the soft tongues and discarded the hard ones. Rebbe said to them, "Just as you prefer the soft tongues, so too others prefer to hear you speak softly and not harshly."

(Vayikra Rabbah 33:1)

Put this text into your own words. What is meant by the second half of the statement? Can you think of an example of when you had to pay the price for negative words you have used?

In ancient as well as contemporary literature, the tongue is often compared to a "double edged sword." The above texts tell us the same thing—a tongue can be an instrument of good or evil, depending on a how a person uses it.

What is an example of something a "good" or "soft" tongue would say? A "bad" or "hard" tongue?

A good tongue would say	_____
A bad tongue would say	_____
A hard tongue would say	_____
A soft tongue would say	_____

 Think about the way your mouth is constructed. You have a *lashon*, a tongue, which allows you to form words. But the tongue is hidden behind two *gedarim*, or "fences," through which the words must pass in order to be heard. These *gedarim* are your teeth and lips.

What can we learn from this about sh'mirat halashon, or watching what we say?

You Can't Take Them Back

The Chafetz Chayyim would exact a promise from rabbis that they would be as careful to refrain from gossiping and slandering as they were not to eat pork. He went on to write a two-hundred page book based on Jewish sources outlining the seriousness of the sin of gossiping. The work was entitled "Chafetz Chayyim," and it was based on the biblical verse (Tehillim 34:13-14): *"Who is the person that desires life, and loves days, that he may see good therein? Keep your tongue from evil, and your lips from speaking guile."*

Following is a Chassidic tale about a person who would often slander:

Once upon a time, there was a man who said unkind things to his neighbors about the town's rabbi. Later, he felt very sorry for what he had done. He begged the rabbi for forgiveness. The rabbi agreed but, the rabbi told him to take several feather pillows from his home, cut them open and scatter the feathers to the winds.

The man did as the rabbi asked and, as he did, the feathers scattered everywhere. Some went over the houses. Others were carried down the street by the wind. Some were tossed into bushes and still others seemed to disappear entirely.

"Now will you forgive me?" asked the man.

"Yes, I will forgive you," answered the rabbi, "as soon as you gather up all of the feathers."

"But that's impossible!" cried the man, pointing to rooftops and streets and bushes and trees.

"Exactly," responded the rabbi. "When we speak badly about someone, the damage spreads just like the feathers, far and wide. It is impossible to fully take back what we have said."

This story clearly demonstrates the severe damage that can be done by a person gossiping, a common occurrence in everyday life.

- *What lessons can we learn from this story?*
- *Has someone ever said something about you that spread like the feathers? How did you feel?*
- *Have you ever said something about someone else that had the same effect?*
- *Even if you can't take them back, are there other ways to make up for harmful words?*
- *What if the man in this story had said good things?*

Words are powerful, and they can do a lot of good, but also a lot of damage. Because of this, we must take care in how we use them. The two "barriers" that surround our tongue, which can be both an instrument of good and of evil, help to ensure that we think twice about the consequences of our words before we speak.

Activity: Are you ready for the challenge?

Challenge: Do not gossip about friends for the next 24 hours. Too long? Try for the next ten hours? Too long? See how long you can go without gossiping.

Agree with your friends to not gossip and agree on the length of time that you will all be gossip-free. Decide on what will happen if (or when) someone does – perhaps he has to run a lap, or give a dollar to *tzedakah*, or maybe she has to do 20 pushups or go an hour without talking or texting. At the conclusion of the time period, get back together with the same group of friends and reflect on how it felt not to gossip.

Does this challenge appeal to you? Why or why not? What role does gossip play in your life? If you didn't gossip, what would you talk about with your friends? How would that change your relationships?

The following are some rabbinic suggestions to help keep people from misusing language:

1. A person should try to discipline himself not to speak too much so that he should not come to the point of uttering lashon hara or indecent words and should not become a chronic complainer. He should, rather, stress silence. (Menorat Hamaor, chapter on lashon hara)

2. A person should always keep a civil tongue in his head, whether he is engaged in the study of Torah or discussing affairs of the world. (Menorat Hamaor, chapter on lashon hara)

3. If one hears something unseemly, one should put one's hands in one's ears. (Ketubot 5a-b)

Activity: Campaign for Shmirat Halashon

You are student council president and a situation breaks out in your school where rumors concerning a certain student are getting out of hand. The student no longer feels comfortable at school. You begin a campaign for Shmirat Halashon.

What are some ways you can stop gossip? How would you promote a gossip-free environment at school when you know it is natural for people to talk?

What Can You Do?

What can you do if you do hear something about someone and don't know what's true and what's false?

1. If you hear something and don't know what's factual or not, don't share it.
2. If your friends are going to discuss someone else, do not use names.
3. Ask yourself if it's really your business to be talking about someone else before you say something
4. Put yourself in that person's place. Would you want someone saying those things about you?
5. If you hear something, remind the speaker that this information may be false and shouldn't be repeated.
6. Ask yourself: "are my words going to have consequences" (ie. hurt someone else)? If yes, practice Shmirat Halashon (guarding your tongue) and don't say it.
7. If someone starts gossiping while you're sitting with them, tell them you're not comfortable talking about other people and change the subject. It's difficult, but you'll feel much better about it.
8. Avoid "friends" who sit around gossiping about others. If they're talking about everyone else, they're likely going to talk about you and aren't worth being friends.

Shmirat Halashon: It's what you say and how you say it.

As we have noted above, the words you choose have a powerful effect on yourself, your relationships and others around you. By watching your words and how they are expressed, you can turn the harmful to helpful. You can choose to love with your words or destroy.

כל המלבין פני חבירו ברבים כאילו שופך   Shaming another in public is akin to murder
דמים   (Talmud Baba Metzia, 58B)

How is embarrassing someone like killing them?

If someone is embarrassed, he usually reacts physically. Some blush, and the blood rushing to their faces is as if you have "spilled" their blood; some turn white, the pallor of death.

The Power of Words
Look at the following. What feelings do they evoke? What do they mean to you?

She's a slut.
What a homo.
He's a loser.
That's so gay.
What a fatty.

What do our harsh words truly mean? When someone refers to a girl as a "slut" or a guy as "so gay," what exactly do these names say about that person?

Scenario 4:
David and Ben were hanging out shooting hoops after school one day. David takes the lay-up and as he's coming down, bumps Ben, knocking him down. "Hey, Homo," Ben says, "Watch where you are going!"

Do you use words like "homo" and "fag" among your friends? How do you think these words affect those who may be struggling with these feelings? Those who may already have acknowledged having such feelings?

How you say it: Cursing
Think about it: some curse words are banned on broadcast television. However, you'll hear anything and everything uttered on cable TV or in the movies. Do you think there should be language laws for televised programming? What about online?

Should we find ways to limit or eliminate swearing at USY conventions? What should the consequences be? Do you think people would be more cautious of their words and guard their tongues more if a policy were in place?

What words could you use in place of curse words? You're still saying the same thing, but not in the same way. How does this change your message?

Examples: "She's being such a *#@$%" could be _____

"I feel like %#$@ today" could be I feel _____

"I'm so #@$% tired" could be _____

Communication is not only what you say, but also how and when you say it. Non-verbal communication like body language, context and tone can all make an impact, either positive or negative, beyond just what words you are saying.

Take this phrase: "Yeah, she is really smart."

First, say it as it is written.
Now, say it with sarcasm.

- *How does the way you say it change its meaning?*
- *Can you think of other examples where tone or context can change the meaning of the words?*
- *In what other ways can body language or non-verbal communication contribute to the meaning of your words?*

Activity: Things I say and Things I do

How do your words reflect your actions?
Fill in the chart below to determine how what you say reflects what you do:

WORDS	ACTIONS
I respect my parents	I help around the house without being asked.

Why do our words have such an impact on us?
How can the way we speak really impact the way we think about and behave toward other people?

- *There are quite a number of musical groups that use so called "foul" language in their songs?*
- *How do you feel about the use of such language?*
- *When you have a family, would you want your own children to be listening to the music of such groups?*
- *Think of some obscene words. How many of them deal with a part of the body or a bodily function? Why are these words considered profane?*
- *When do you find that people most use profanity? Is there a reason for its use at these times?*
- *Are there ways of modifying your language to a more acceptable form?*

An Anti-Profanity Campaign

Jewish tradition has suggested that a person try to avoid hearing foul language from others. For example, in the Talmud (Ketubot 5a-b) it says: "If one hears something improper, he should put his fingers in his ears." Choose a partner and compose a list of other things that people who are concerned with misuse and abuse of language can do to fight back against those who use profanity and lashon hara.

Click! Words you can't get back
Shmirat Halashon and Online Communication

How does technology contribute to spreading rumors, gossip, and bad-mouthing about others? In what ways can someone be shamed in public through technology? How can technology be more dangerous than school gossip? What do you do to protect yourself from technological lashon hara?

Just because you are communicating through technology doesn't mean the words and their effects aren't real. In the age of instant access, we often take communication for granted. It is so easy to send a message to someone in a hundred different ways. Sometimes we use technology to say what we would be too embarrassed to say to someone's face. These messages should not be treated any differently than face to face communication. In fact, because these messages can be spread immediately to an unlimited number of people, we must be even more careful with our words.

According to "Sex and Tech" a survey on teenage sexuality and digital media use
(653 teens surveyed) 89% of teens have a profile on a social-networking site like MySpace ® or Facebook ® and 84% of teens are "texting."

Scenario 5: Face Off

Hannah came home from a recent convention excited about the weekend. She had made a lot of friends and couldn't wait to update her status on Facebook® Hannah logged on to her computer and moments later burst into tears. Melanie had posted a simple status update on her Facebook® page: "Hannah hooked up with Steve!"

Was this news Melanie's to share?
How do you think Hannah felt because Melanie shared the news?
Does it elevate someone's status to reveal gossip about others?
If Hannah or Steve had posted it first, would it be okay to comment on it?

Is watching what you say the same as watching what you post or type? In today's world, given the primary nature of the way we communicate via technology, should we consider a new term for Shmirat Halashon—Shmirat Ha'etzba'ot (guarding your typing fingers)?

Digital Gossip

Everyone is in a state of constant communication and we're sharing and communicating more than ever before. But, while technology is great, the downside to communicating this way is that once its been freed from your fingertips, the whole world can 'hear' what you said.

Have you ever posted or sent anything that you wish you could get back?
Have you ever misdirected a message by accident?

SEXTING

Although most teens and young adults who send sexually suggestive content are sending it to their significant other (boyfriend or girlfriend), others say they are sending such material to those they want to "hook up" with or to someone they only know online.

Read these statistics and discuss:
One in five teen girls and one in ten younger teen girls (age 13 to 16) have electronically sent or posted nude or semi-nude photos or videos of themselves. Even more teen girls, 37 percent, have sent or posted sexually suggestive text, email or IM (instant messages).

More than half of teen girls (51 percent) say pressure from a guy is a reason girls send sexy messages or images, and 18 percent of teen boys say pressure from a girl is a reason.

Why do you think these teens are engaging in this activity? How do you think it impacts the way they regard themselves? What do you think are some short term consequences? What do you think are some long term consequences? What role does the concept of *kedusha* have in this activity?

Activity: Text-ercise

Do you say more in a text message than you would to someone's face? The newest teen danger "sexting," where teens send sexually explicit text messages to one another, illustrates how we are less inhibited to say things using technology than we would to face-to-face.

Try looking through your text message "sent messages" folder at some of the text messages you've sent recently to friends. Would you want you mom/dad/teacher/principal to see these messages? Delete the ones you wouldn't want them to see as a sign of commitment to Shmirat Ha'etzbaot/ Shmirat HaLashon.

People post more online than they would say in real life to real people because they don't face immediate consequences and are located in a "safe space." Because you can't get anything back once it's been sent, are you more cautious of what you post online?

Think about it: Is the word "send," a dangerous word?

How can you apply the concepts of shmirat ha'lashon, to how you use MySpace®, Facebook®, Twitter® and other forms of digital social media?

Next time you're about to send a message STOP! Ask yourself —is this something I would say to his or her face? Is it something worth saying? Does it need to be said? How will I feel if other people read it? More importantly, how will my friend feel if this message 'goes viral'? Would I want a trusted adult in my life to see this? If I apply for a camp job this summer and the director checks my Facebook® page, would he/she find anything? If you have any doubts, then don't send it or post it.

Scenario 6: From Friend to Send

Emily, Jessica and Jordana were sitting in the backseat of the car on their way home from a recent program. Emily was messaging back and forth with Jonathan from her cell phone. The three were silent, except for the sound of fingers flying over the keyboard of Emily's cell phone. Text, text, pause, silence. Then, a jingle as a new text announced its arrival and all three girls start laughing as they read the text message from Jon. Jon wasn't aware that Jessica and Jordana were reading his texts.

Was it okay for Emily to share Jonathan's text message with Jessica and Jordana?

Scenario 7: Accidental Exposure

Michelle and her girlfriends were hanging out in the locker room at school following their soccer practice. One of her friends started making funny faces and the girls thought it was hysterical. Jennifer took out her cell phone to capture the moment with her phone's camera. That night, Jennifer posted the pictures from the afternoon on her home page without looking at them too closely. Michelle called her horrified a few hours later when her mother saw the pictures and noticed that Michelle was only in her underwear.

Was it okay for Jennifer to post pictures of her friends?
What do you need to consider before allowing photos to be taken of you?
What are the dangers of posting pictures on a social networking site?
What are your responsibilities as the person posting pictures?

FIVE THINGS TO THINK ABOUT BEFORE PRESSING "SEND"

Don't assume anything you send or post is going to remain private.
Your messages and images will get passed around, even if you think they won't: 40% of teens and young adults say they have had a sexually suggestive message (originally meant to be private) shown to them and 20% say they have shared such a message with someone other than the person for whom is was originally meant.

There is no changing your mind in cyberspace—anything you send or post will never truly go away.
Something that seems fun and flirty and is done on a whim will never really die. Potential employers, college recruiters, teachers, coaches, parents, friends, enemies, strangers and others may all be able to find your past posts, even after you delete them. And it is nearly impossible to control what other people are posting about you. Think about it: Even if you have second thoughts and delete a racy photo, there is no telling who has already copied that photo and posted it elsewhere.

Don't give in to the pressure to do something that makes you uncomfortable, even in cyberspace.
More than 40% of teens and young adults (42% total, 47% of teens, 38% of young adults) say "pressure from guys" is a reason girls and women send and post sexually suggestive messages and images. More than 20% of teens and young adults (22% total, 24% of teens, 20% of young adults) say "pressure from friends" is a reason guys send and post sexually suggestive messages and images.

Consider the recipient's reaction.
Just because a message is meant to be fun doesn't mean the person who gets it will see it that way. Four in ten teen girls who have sent sexually suggestive content did so "as a joke" but many teen boys (29%) say that girls who send such content are "expected to date or hook up in real life." It's easier to be more provocative or outgoing online, but whatever you write, post or send does contribute to the real life impression you're making.

Nothing is truly anonymous.
Nearly one in five young people who send sexually suggestive messages and images send to people they only know online (18% total, 15% of teens, 19% of young adults). It is important to remember that even if people only know you by screen name, online profile, phone number or email address, that they can probably find you if they try hard enough.

(Excerpted from Sex and Tech, ©2009, The National Campaign to Prevent Teen and Unplanned Pregnancy.)

Actions Have Consequences

There was a man who was friendly with a man named Kamtza, but who was an enemy of Bar-Kamtza. He made a feast and said to his servant, "Go and bring Kamtza to my feast," but the servant brought Bar-Kamtza instead.

The one who made the feast found Bar-Kamtza seated there. He said to him, "Since you are my enemy, what are you doing here? Get up and get out!" Bar-Kamtza said, "Since I'm here already, let me stay so that I will not be shamed in front of all these guests, and I will pay you for what I eat and drink."

The host refused. Bar-Kamtza offered to pay for the entire meal; the host still refused. In front of all the guests, the host threw Bar-Kamtza out of the house.

Bar-Kamtza was so angry at the host, he went to the Caesar, King of Rome, who ruled over the Jews at this time. Bar-Kamtza told the Caesar that the Jews were rebelling against him; this act leads to the destruction of the Second Temple by the Romans.

Rabbi Elazar says: Come and see the tremendous negative impact of embarrassing someone, for it destroyed the Temple.

What happens in this story?
How could the host have handled this situation differently?
How could Bar-Kamtza have handled this situation differently?
What role do the guests play in this story?
Think back to the story about the two brothers, and how the Temple was built on those grounds because of their unconditional love for each other. Why does the story we just read cause the destruction of the Temple?

Guard My Tongue

יד נְצֹר לְשׁוֹנְךָ מֵרָע; וּשְׂפָתֶיךָ, מִדַּבֵּר מִרְמָה. 14 Keep your tongue from evil, and your lips from speaking lie.

(Tehillim 34:14)

Why doesn't it say "guard your tongue from evil speech?"

Every day when we say the Amidah, we make reference to the idea that it is difficult to guard our speech at all times and difficult to be the subject of rumor. At the conclusion of the Amidah, we recite a personal prayer, based on a prayer of Mar Bar Ravina in Talmud Berachot 17a:

אֱלֹהַי, נְצֹר לְשׁוֹנִי מֵרָע, וּשְׂפָתַי מִדַּבֵּר מִרְמָה, וְלִמְקַלְלַי נַפְשִׁי תִדֹּם, וְנַפְשִׁי כֶּעָפָר לַכֹּל תִּהְיֶה.

My God, keep my tongue from evil, my lips from lies. Help me ignore those who slander me. Let me be humble before all....

Our words need to be carefully chosen.

The rabbis have said that a slanderer's crime is worse than that of a murderer. What are some ways that language can create greater harm to a person than physical injury?

What is your opinion of the advice that the rabbis present to avoid the misuse of language?
If you were a teacher teaching this to your students, what personal advice would you have for them?

Shmirat Halashon: Rules to live by/Communication 101

It's not what you say, it's how you say it—communicate with kind words, present yourself to others as intellectual and respectful.

Do you agree that "it's not what you say?" Does that mean that you can still say inappropriate remarks as long as you do so with smart word choices?

א לַכֹּל, זְמָן; וְעֵת לְכָל-חֵפֶץ, תַּחַת הַשָּׁמָיִם.

ז עֵת לִקְרוֹעַ וְעֵת לִתְפּוֹר,
עֵת לַחֲשׁוֹת וְעֵת לְדַבֵּר.

1 To every thing there is a season, and a time to every purpose under the heaven:

7 A time to rend, and a time to sew;
a time to keep silence, and a time to speak;

(Kohelet 3:1, 7)

- *Do you agree?*
- *Why do you think "silence" comes before "speaking?"*
- *Is it harder to say something, or to refrain from saying something?*
- *Can you think of an instance where remaining silent could be a bad thing?*

Activity: The Ten second rule

Apply the ten second rule—before you respond to a potentially offensive remark, pause for 10 seconds to give yourself time to think about how you are going to respond.

Try it! Someone makes fun of the new jacket you just bought. Use the ten second rule and the "it's how you say it" rule to reply. What was your immediate response (that you didn't say). What did you say after using the ten second rule? What was the difference between the two responses? Which one was the better choice? Why?

In this chapter we discussed the power of words and the way they can affect our relationships. We learned that the mitzvah of *shmirat ha'lashon*, guarding our tongue, is an extremely important mitzvah, though very difficult to keep. We discussed the ways that online communication has the power to spread rumors very quickly and that it is important to think before pressing 'send'. We acknowledged that we may be more careless in what we say online than in what we say in person. Curse words and foul language have no place in our speech and we tried to think of different ways to express ourselves. Finally, we thought about ways to communicate our feelings that will help us resolve rather than reinforce difficulties in our relationships. We know that being able to communicate and disagree are important elements of healthy relationships.

וְאָהַבְתָּ לְרֵעֲךָ כָּמוֹךָ 99

Part Three

בֵּין אָדָם לַחֲבֵרוֹ
Bein Adam L'chavero
Between Friends

What do you think makes a healthy relationship?

Activity: Components of a healthy relationship

 From 1-4, label which of the four components of a healthy relationship are the most important to you. Although you have prioritized the four components, give an example for each as to why a healthy relationship cannot exist without each of the four.

___Respect
Mutual respect
Respect for opinions, feelings and decisions
A healthy relationship can not exist without respect because:

___Equality in all aspects of the relationship
Equality of power
Freedom of emotional expression
Both partners feel in charge of their own emotions and actions
A healthy relationship can not exist without equality because:

___Communication
Honest and open communication
Freedom to express opinions
Ability to disagree and work out problems
Compromise, but not on a partner's values
A healthy relationship can not exist without communication because:

___Love
Grounded in friendship
Based on mutual respect and trust
Don't have to "earn" it
A healthy relationship can not exist without love because:

A healthy relationship is dependent upon all of the above categories, but is rooted in friendship.

Activity: Healthy Relationships Free Association

What words come to your mind when you hear someone say "healthy relationship?"

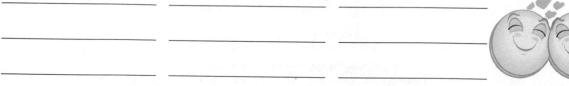

_____   _____   _____

_____   _____   _____

_____   _____   _____

Look at the following list of words:

control	love	compromise	support
anger	respect	distrust	honesty
equality	friendship	communication	stalking
trust	violence	fighting	hurt
loyalty	compassion	disrespect	safety

Which words did you think of? Which words did you forget?
Write the words that are part of a healthy relationship in the full heart, and the words that represent an unhealthy relationship in the broken heart. Feel free to add any of your own words.

Were there any words you had trouble placing, or that you thought could go in both hearts?
Do some characteristics belong in a healthy relationship, but only in conjunction with other characteristics? What does a healthy relationship look like?

What does a healthy relationship look like?

Chapter Eight
Dating

- *How are dating relationships and friendship connected?*
- *Can you love your friends without feeling romantic love? What's the difference?*
- *Can you be "just friends" with someone you are romantically attracted to?*
- *Can you be friends with someone who is of the opposite sex without it being romantic?*
- *Can you be friends with someone of the same sex without it being romantic?*
- *What happens when you take friendship to the next level?*
- *When does it become more than friends?*

The ability to experience close friendships is often the first step toward understanding more significant relationships later in life.

Activity: Are you ready to be in a romantic relationship?

Start by taking this simple relationship test. For each question, please write down a number between 1-5— 1 is ABSOLUTELY NOT; 2 is NOT YET; 3 is MAYBE; 4 is PROBABLY and 5 is DEFINITELY

_____Do I know who I am and what I want in a relationship?

_____Do I have the time and energy to give to another person?

_____Am I willing to listen when my partner wants to discuss something —even if it means not watching my favorite show or missing a chance to hang out with friends?

_____Do I want to help my partner feel secure and comfortable regardless of the situation we're in?

_____Can I handle problems and make safe, responsible decisions?

_____Can I stand up for my values and beliefs, even if my partner disagrees?

_____Am I able to keep promises and things told to me in confidence?

_____Can I/ do I want to prioritize someone else's needs above my own?

_____Am I ready to share my thoughts, feelings, and emotions with another person?

Add up your score. What did you find out?

Activity: "He's Just a friend"—"He's more than a friend"

Define, in your own words, the following:

friend of the opposite sex _____

"Friend with Benefits" _____

Best Friend _____

Holding hands _____

Lover _____

Partner _____

"Hooking up" _____

In a Relationship _____

"Seeing each other" _____

Dating _____

In today's world, pressure to date, if not dating itself, begins in the teenage years. High school students often forge meaningful and significant relationships with others their age that become an integral part of their respective lives. It may be a time when the realization that the expectation to date someone of the opposite sex doesn't fit. Each Jewish teenager should create a dating ethic. Two considerations demonstrate the need to create such an ethic, that is, a set of rules for making good decisions.

First, one should be consciously aware that while only a minority of people end up marrying their high school sweetheart, some people in fact do end up doing exactly that. As such, for any teenager to assume that one's relationship with one's partner is short-term, might in fact simply be a mistake. There are those who date the same person from high school through college and beyond, even though perhaps separated by significant distances during the courtship. Not every teenage romance is short-lived. It is not unheard of that a couple might form the foundation of a lasting and serious relationship while in high school.

For the majority of people however, teenage relationships do not lead directly to commitments or marriage. As such, it might fairly be asked what impact, if any, a teenager's dating ethic has upon family structure. While several possibilities might soundly respond to this question, one answer seems to clearly evolve from classical Rabbinic thought.

בֶּן עַזַּאי אוֹמֵר, הֱוֵי רָץ לְמִצְוָה קַלָּה (כְּבַחֲמוּרָה), וּבוֹרֵחַ מִן הָעֲבֵרָה. שֶׁמִּצְוָה גּוֹרֶרֶת מִצְוָה, וַעֲבֵרָה גוֹרֶרֶת עֲבֵרָה. שֶׁשְּׂכַר מִצְוָה, מִצְוָה. וּשְׂכַר עֲבֵרָה, עֲבֵרָה:

Ben Azzai said: One should run to fulfill a minor commandment as if it were a major one and flee from any transgression; for one mitzvah leads to another mitzvah, while one sin leads to yet another sin. The reward for doing a mitzvah is another mitzvah while the reward for one sin is yet another sin.

(Pirkei Avot 4:2)

According to this mishnah, humans are creatures of habit. Psychological studies have repeatedly shown that past behavior is the best predictor of future performance. Just as New Year's resolutions are quickly forgotten, we tend to repeat the behaviors that we have already engaged in. The type of person who you say is okay to date today is more than likely to have an impact on the type of person who you think is okay to date in the future when more serious relationships develop. As such, even one's earliest dating patterns play a significant role in influencing one's future and the future of one's family.

As with any other important pursuit, the preparation affects the final result. If working hard at practices results in a better played game, if doing homework results in a particular type of grade, if being a good person makes the world a better place, then certainly, who and how you date today can affect who you marry tomorrow.

In any dating situation decisions must be made which impact profoundly upon one's life. Who one decides to date and the type of relationship which one decides to pursue will have consequences. It would be wise for anyone dating or considering dating to thoughtfully assess where the results of his or her decisions might lead. The important thing about dating is that we learn how to build and sustain intimate relationships. We learn to give of ourselves, to compromise, to listen, to empathize, to love, and to be honest. We learn to express difficult emotions, to take risks, etc.

Through dating, we discover what is important to us in a relationship, and what is important to others. If the dating relationship is so important, how can we be sure we're looking for the right person? If there are plenty of fish in the sea, how do I know which one to catch? The following midrash illustrates the question of "meant to be":

A [Roman] matron asked R. Jose: "In how many days did the Holy One, blessed is God, create God's world?" "In six days," he answered. "Then what has God been doing since then?" "God sits and makes matches," he answered, "assigning this man to that woman, and this woman to that man." "If that is difficult," she gibed, "I too can do the same." She went and matched [her slaves], giving this man to that woman, this woman to that man and so on. Some time after those who were thus united went and beat one another, this woman saying, "I do not want this man: while this man protested, "I do not want that woman." Straightway she summoned R. Jose b. Halafta and admitted to him: "There is no god like your God: it is true, your Torah is indeed beautiful and praiseworthy, and you spoke the truth!"

(Bereishit Rabbah 68:4)

As the Roman noblewoman in the story discovered, finding your *bashert* (literally, predestined, this usually refers to your soul mate or the person God intends you to marry) is not as simple as some movies may have us believe. Whether or not you believe in love at first sight, a lot goes into choosing a partner.

A healthy dating relationship is rooted in friendship. Previously, we examined both the joys and "oys" of friendship. Now, let's look at romantic relationships in the same way.

How are friendships and dating relationships similar? _____

How are friendships and dating relationships different? _____

What characteristics do you look for in a dating partner? _____

_____

_____

What is the distinction between loving your best friend and loving a dating partner?

Look back at the chapter on friendships, at the list of characteristics that you look for in a friend. Do you see any similarities? Differences?

Activity: Friends vs. Romance

In one column, list the characteristics of good friendships. In the second column, list characteristics of romantic relationships. Next, compare the lists and circle the similarities.

Good Friendships	Romantic Relationships

What is complicated about the relationship of "just friends."

Naturally, Judaism has a lot to say about the subject of choosing a partner. In the source below, we are encouraged to find a partner who is of a similar age:

שאם היה הוא ילד והיא זקנה, הוא זקן
והיא ילדה, אומרין לו : מה לך אצל ילדה,
מה לך אצל זקנה, כלך אצל שכמותך ואל
תשים קטטה בביתך לא צריכא

If he, for instance, was young and she old, or if he was old and she was young, he is told, "What would you with a young woman?" or "What would you with an old woman?" "Go to one who is [of the same age] as yourself and create no strife in your house!"

(Talmud, Tractate Yevamot 44a)

This suggests that greater compatibility is found between those who are at similar stages of life. While popular culture has often stated that opposites attract, many relationships are formed because people share similar backgrounds and therefore similar values and experiences.

In the past, you may have been interested in establishing a close relationship with another person. When you have been interested in someone, what has that interest been based on? Looks? Personality? Intelligence?

What first attracted you to these other people?

Look at your answer above. Now, think about the qualities you want in the person who you might eventually marry. Are the qualities the same as those that attracted you to other people? Why or why not?

Judaism also had its own version of the "Dating Game" where singles could meet each other:

אָמַר רַבָּן שִׁמְעוֹן בֶּן גַּמְלִיאֵל, לֹא הָיוּ יָמִים טוֹבִים לְיִשְׂרָאֵל כַּחֲמִשָּׁה עָשָׂר בְּאָב וּכְיוֹם הַכִּפּוּרִים, שֶׁבָּהֶן בְּנוֹת יְרוּשָׁלַיִם יוֹצְאוֹת בִּכְלֵי לָבָן שְׁאוּלִין, שֶׁלֹּא לְבַיֵּשׁ אֶת מִי שֶׁאֵין לוֹ. כָּל הַכֵּלִים טְעוּנִין טְבִילָה. וּבְנוֹת יְרוּשָׁלַיִם יוֹצְאוֹת וְחוֹלוֹת בַּכְּרָמִים. וּמֶה הָיוּ אוֹמְרוֹת, בָּחוּר, שָׂא נָא עֵינֶיךָ וּרְאֵה, מָה אַתָּה בוֹרֵר לָךְ. אַל תִּתֵּן עֵינֶיךָ בַּנּוֹי, תֵּן עֵינֶיךָ בַּמִּשְׁפָּחָה. (משלי לא)

Rabban Shimon ben Gamliel said, There were no holidays for Israel as the fifteenth of Av (Tu b'Av) and as Yom Kippur, for on them the daughters of Jerusalem go forth in borrowed white garments, so as not to embarrass whoever does not have... And the daughters of Jerusalem go forth and dance in the vineyards. And what would they say? "Young man, lift up your eyes and see, what you choose for yourself. Do not set your eyes on beauty, set your eyes on the family: 'Grace is deceitful, and beauty is vain, but a woman that fears the Lord, she shall be praised' (Prov. 31:30).
(Mishnah, Tractate Ta'anit 4:8)

Do you think that wealth, beauty and status should even be considered when choosing a partner, or should they be off limits? Why?

It is interesting to note that rather than promoting the cultural ideal of "keeping up with the Joneses" this text emphasizes attributes other than wealth and physical beauty. The suitors are encouraged to consider how the woman was raised and the values that she holds.

In what ways could partners from different family backgrounds have issues that come up specifically because of those differences?

You have gone through your own list of qualities that you would look for in a potential mate. *How does your list compare with those that these texts seem to be concentrating on?*

Do you agree with the Jewish ideas of who is a good person to marry and who is not?

The text above seems to be describing a singles event from about 2,000 years ago. *What are the advantages and disadvantages of choosing a spouse quickly, but without knowing background information such as financial or family status?*

While there is room for latitude in dating, certain standards are fundamental in Judaism. Rabbi Elliot Dorff addressed many of these issues in "This is My Beloved, This is My Friend: A Rabbinic Letter on Intimate Relations." Three messages are clear about dating within Judaism:

1. Jewish law forbids intermarriage without exception. This bears upon a Jew's dating ethic; dating only Jews enhances the potential of a Jewish marriage and raising Jewish children. While no legal code explicitly forbids dating non-Jews, this is because such activity is not entertained in Jewish law as a legitimate option.

2. As the most intimate and holy of acts, intercourse is reserved for the most intimate and holy relationships. Ultimate intimacy is tied to ultimate commitment and therefore, marriage is the appropriate context for sexual intercourse. From a Jewish perspective full commitment and the development of the emotional and spiritual relationship must precede physical intimacy.

3. Every person, male or female, must not be objectified, but rather treated as a valued soul, created in the image of God. To treat a partner, a date, or indeed anyone without expressing the highest concern for that person's integrity and inherent holiness is nothing less then a sin.

Rabbi Dorff adds a special message concerning teenagers:

If the above considerations apply to adults, they apply all the more to teenagers, for whom the commitments of marriage and children are simply not possible. This, though, puts such people in an especially difficult bind, for the level of sexual hormones in their bodies is as high as it will ever get. We rabbis recognize that teenagers throughout history have been driven by their hormones to seek each other's company and to explore their sexuality. The Conservative Movement has therefore created, and will continue to create, opportunities for Jewish teenagers to meet each other and to learn to feel comfortable in each other's presence. As long as the relationship is voluntary on the part of both partners, and as long as Judaism's norms of modesty and privacy are maintained, holding hands, hugging, and kissing are as legitimate for teenagers as they build romantic relationships as they are for older people....

One other matter.... we want to reaffirm here our belief that Jewish teenagers should date Jews exclusively. As much as marriage may seem eons away, dating is the usual way in which young people meet and ultimately marry. Marrying the boy or girl next door is still a common phenomenon, for such people share experiences from their high school years and perhaps even from early childhood, and so high school students need to restrict their dates to Jews.

Along the same lines, high school juniors and seniors planning for college should be sure to choose a school with a significant number of Jews. That is important for general religious, educational, and social reasons, but the romantic factor is absolutely critical. Many people do not find their mate in college, but a significant number do, and so one important element in a Jew's choice of college should be the availability of other Jews with whom one can form a community and among whom one can date.

("This is My Beloved, This is My Friend: A Rabbinic Letter on Intimate Relations," by Rabbi Elliot N. Dorff, A Paper of The Commission on Human Sexuality, The Rabbinical Assembly, 1996, page 36, Used with permission.)

Judaism clearly places a priority on finding a partner, but not everyone chooses to marry or enter a lifelong commitment. Why do you think that some people stay single? What would Jewish tradition say about people who stayed single?

How should the Jewish community reach out to single Jews?

There are several Internet-based dating services designed for Jews to meet other Jews. How do you feel about this method of meeting?

Some Jewish groups organize "shidduchim" or matches for single Jews. How do you feel about this?

If your friend says he's opposed to intermarriage but decided to inter-date anyway, at what point in the relationship should he disclose the fact that he would not intermarry?

There are those who say that they would never intermarry, but think that inter-dating is OK because there is no intent at the time of the date to get married. Although dating does not always lead to marriage, there is an expectation that it could lead to a serious relationship and to some long-term commitment to an exclusive relationship (perhaps months or even years). If a friend decided to inter-date, would you counsel her to disclose her preference about intermarriage at the beginning of the relationship? Should she say to her date: "I'd like to go out with you and get to know you, but we can't get serious because I will only marry someone who is Jewish."?

In any dating situation decisions must be made which impact profoundly upon one's life. Who one decides to date and the type of relationship which one decides to pursue will have consequences. It would be wise for anyone dating or considering dating to thoughtfully assess where the results of his or her decisions might lead.

Activity: Thinking It Through

Each of us has set limits about who we will and will not date.

WOULD YOU DATE SOMEONE WHO?	WHAT ARE THE CONSEQUENCES?
Lives in another city?	
Insists on seeing you at least three times every week?	
Your parents do not approve of, for whatever reason?	
Your friends do not approve of, for whatever reason?	
Is in college now?	
Whose code of morality (right and wrong) is different from your own?	
Is less observant than you?	
Is more observant than you?	
Won't eat in your parent's house because it is not kosher?	
Goes to synagogue on a daily basis?	
Whose religion is different from your religion?	
Never goes or has no interest in going to synagogue?	
Refuses to give money to beggars on the street?	
Refuses to fast on Yom Kippur?	
Sees serious sexual activity as a necessary part of your relationship?	
Feels that physical intimacy should be left to the confines of marriage?	
Does not respect you as a Jew?	

Dating in Hollywood

How does Hollywood define friendship vs. romantic love? Think of two movies where the lines between friendship and romantic love become blurred. In a heterosexual couple, can a man and woman be "just friends?"

Made of Honor- Patrick Dempsey (2008)- Hannah asks Tom, her best friend to be her "maid of honor," but between the bridal shower and bad hair days, he realizes that he would rather be the man standing next to her as the groom.

When Harry Met Sally- Billy Crystal, Meg Ryan (1989). Harry and Sally are close friends and they both enjoy having a friend of the opposite sex. The problem is, though, can a heterosexual man and a woman be "just friends?"

When It Turns to Love

Physical intimacy often distinguishes friendship from "more than friends" or romantic partnership. Physical intimacy can also greatly complicate a friendship as it blurs the lines between friendship and a romantic partnership and can often mislead one of the partners if intentions are not clear. Although romantic relationships are confusing and often difficult to define, in the Jewish tradition, romantic partnership, which includes intimacy, is rooted first and foremost in friendship and respect.

Loving Your Neighbor: Love and Physical Intimacy

The fifth bracha of the Sheva Brachot recited at a wedding meal:

שַׂמֵּחַ תְּשַׂמַּח רֵעִים הָאֲהוּבִים, כְּשַׂמֵּחֲךָ יְצִירְךָ בְּגַן עֵדֶן מִקֶּדֶם

Grant perfect joy to these <u>loving companions</u>, as You did to the first man and woman in the Garden of Eden.

Notice the underlined words. The word *loving* is paired with the word *companions. Why?*

זֶה דוֹדִי וְזֶה רֵעִי   This is my beloved, this is my friend.

(Song of Songs 5:16)

Why does the word "friend" follow the word "beloved?" What is this text telling us?

What is the common theme or idea of both texts? What do we recognize from both of these texts, popularly found on many wedding invitations or on the cover of wedding benchers?

In order for one to love another romantically, he/she must first and foremost love him/her as a friend. But how?

Rabbi Elliot Dorff explains how love is rooted in friendship in his previously mentioned publication on intimate relationships. Using a list of basic Jewish values, Rabbi Dorff presents a Conservative Jewish perspective on physical relationships and presents his argument rooted in values of *B'tzelem Elohim* and *Ve'ahavta L'rayecha Kamocha, Tzniut* and more:

> Returning to our discussion on ve'ahavta l'rayecha kamocha, how do we show our love? If we are to support our friends, the support we show a romantic partner should be even stronger, "this means that in such relationships, we must care for our partner in both feeling and action. Negatively, we may not offend or annoy him or her, take him or her for granted and certainly not harm him or him in any way. Positively, love requires that we think of the other's needs and wants in living our own lives and that we make a point of attending to them."

> Every relationship will inevitably have anger, conflict and fighting, even healthy ones. If someone is upset and feels unable to express feelings and emotions, this is not healthy. But anger, conflict and fighting must be balanced with good communication, compromise and respect for each other's opinions.

Additionally, although compromise is an important healthy relationship characteristic, too much compromise is not good either. If one partner is always compromising while the other one refuses to, or if someone feels like he or she needs to compromise on values or beliefs in order to please a partner, this is not healthy. In order for a relationship to be healthy, one must be able to distinguish between compromise and sacrifice. Respecting one's partner means considering their needs *in addition* to your own needs.

Same-Sex Relationships

In this chapter, we have intentionally not distinguished between male/ female relationships and same-sex relationships. ***Do you think there should be a difference?***

Can there be love between members of the same sex without romance?

Although we have a long way to go, the Jewish community has taken great strides to be more welcoming for same sex couples. ***What steps can we take to be more accepting of love between two people of the same sex?***

Scenario 1:

You are hanging out after school with two friends Ben and Danny. Ben confides in the two of you that he thinks he might be gay and has a crush on your other friend, Jonathan. Danny gets quiet, shuffles his papers around and abruptly gets up to leave. Ben gets really upset and asks you to forget he ever said anything and begs you both not to say a word.

Do you think Danny's reaction to Ben's confession of feelings is typical? What would you do if one of your friends "came out" to you and asked you not to say anything?

Scenario 2:

Judy and Aliza met at the last regional program and have hung out a little since. Judy told Jennifer that she likes Aliza but isn't sure if Aliza feels the same way about her. Jennifer isn't completely sure what to suggest because she has never been asked about a same-sex crush, but encouraged Judy to ask Aliza out. Judy is worried that it may jeopardize her friendship with Aliza.

How can Judy share how she feels without jeopardizing her friendship with Aliza?
What are some ways that Aliza might react?
If you were Jennifer, what would you say to Judy?
What do you think they should do?

Conflict in Dating Relationships

Love is a powerful emotion and whenever loving emotions are present, even the most "ideal" couples face adversity and disagreement. Because conflict is inevitable, some couples find that it is a good idea to have a Problem Solving Plan (PSP) in place to help them work through disagreements. The disagreement might be something as simple as which movie to watch, or as serious as one partner wanting to do something the other is not comfortable with. Having and following a plan to resolve conflict will help ensure that both parties have been able to speak and be heard, and that both feel valued as equal partners in the relationship.

Here is an example of what your plan might include:

My Problem Solving Plan (PSP)
- Both people agree to try and work things out. If one person is too angry to talk, or doesn't want to work things out, there is no way to come to a solution.
- Talk about the issue without using blaming language or name-calling.
- Let both people speak without interruption while the other listens.
- Talk about all potential solutions, even those that may seem impossible or silly. Then, think about the pros and cons of each choice.
- Choose the solution that benefits both parties as equally as possible.

Compromise is an important element of conflict resolution and often partners will need to compromise to come to a solution. However, there is such a thing as too much compromise. If one person feels that he or she is compromising on beliefs or values, or feels he is giving up a lot while the other partner is only gaining, it is probably not a good solution.

- *What are your core values that are not up for negotiation?*
- *Are there things you would not compromise on? How do you know? How do you decide?*
- *Would you have sex if you don't want to have sex and don't think that teens should have sex?*
- *Would you eat non-kosher food if being kosher is integral to who you are?*
- *Would you cheat on a test to help your partner, if one of your core values is being honest?*

Chapter Nine: Ahhhhh... marriage

Marriage, the unity of two souls into one, is unquestionably considered to be the ideal human state within the Jewish tradition. The Torah expresses this thought in the very beginning, when it states (referring to Adam and Eve):

יח וַיֹּאמֶר יְהוָה אֱלֹהִים, לֹא-טוֹב הֱיוֹת הָאָדָם לְבַדּוֹ; אֶעֱשֶׂה-לּוֹ עֵזֶר, כְּנֶגְדּוֹ.

18 It is not good for man to be alone; I will make a fitting helper for him.

(Bereishit 2:18)

כד עַל-כֵּן, יַעֲזָב-אִישׁ, אֶת-אָבִיו, וְאֶת-אִמּוֹ; וְדָבַק בְּאִשְׁתּוֹ, וְהָיוּ לְבָשָׂר אֶחָד.

24 Hence a man leaves his father and mother and clings to his wife, so that they become one flesh.

(Bereishit 2:24)

The Christian Bible, on the other hand, considers celibacy as a higher ideal than marriage, which is a factor driving Christianity's attitude toward the sexual impulse. To some Christians, marriage is thought of as a concession to human weakness; the Rabbis, however, saw celibacy as unnatural. The Talmud says: "He who has no wife is not a proper man." In contrast to the Christian outlook on sex, the Talmud states: "Were it not for the sexual impulse, no man would build a house, marry a wife, or beget children." Thus, not only is marriage acceptable, but it is healthy and necessary for the proper development of human character and maturity.

What do you think "become one flesh" means? Is this a reference to just the physical aspects of marriage?

In our day and age, do you feel that children have already left their parents before marriage?

In what ways can a marriage symbolize a more permanent change in the relationship between a person and his or her parents?

Why do you think Judaism puts such a strong emphasis on marriage?

We can see the importance attached to marriage by our tradition by the use of certain metaphors and imagery. The prophets often referred to the relationship between God and Israel as that between husband and wife. An entire book of the Bible, *Shir HaShirim* (Song of Songs), utilizes explicit sexual imagery, which was later interpreted as a metaphor for the God--Israel relationship.

The *Shabbat* is referred to as a bride in the Friday Evening liturgy. We sing, "*Lecha dodi likrat kallah*—לְכָה דוֹדִי לִקְרַאת כַּלָּה—Come, my beloved, to greet the Sabbath bride."

What about a Jew's relationship with Shabbat would we be trying to duplicate in a marriage?
What sort of parallels can you draw between Shabbat and marriage?

Some religions or philosophies emphasize body over soul or soul over body. Judaism tries to strike a healthy balance, seeing the physical and spiritual as equally valid and important. We can see this

וְאָהַבְתָּ לְרֵעֲךָ כָּמוֹךָ 115

difference demonstrated by the vocabulary of various civilizations. The Greeks had two words for the two possible manifestations of love:

agape—represents the spiritual type of love.
eros—represents the physical type of love.

Hebrew has only one word, *ahava*. In other words, we use the same word to describe our relationship with God as we do for describing sexual attraction. This concretizes the idea that we have always felt an interdependence of the physical and the spiritual, or what some call the profane and the sacred. We believe that the physical world is capable of being raised to a spiritual level, that indeed spirituality is impossible without the tangible, material world. Thus, it should be no surprise that the Hebrew word for marriage is kiddushin, which contains within it the word kadosh—holy or sacred.

Finding a Jewish Partner

Why is it important to find a partner who is Jewish? Our tradition and religion are indeed beautiful, containing numerous treasures.

What about Judaism is important to you that you would want to share with your children?

Think about what in your home makes it Jewish. What sits on the shelves in your home?

What issues do you think you would have to deal with if your partner were not Jewish?

Not unlike other defined ethnic, national, or religious groups, Judaism has always emphasized the importance of "in-marriage." The very fact that statistics of intermarriage are recorded by Jews as well as other groups, attests to the emphasis which is placed on this subject. Again, this is not only a Jewish concern, but a concern of many other groups. While some individuals are certainly not bothered by the phenomenon of intermarriage, it is clear that most groups, be they religions, nationalities, or races, are minimally interested and more likely to be concerned about this reality which occurs frequently within the great North American melting pot.

Given the fact that intermarriage is a reality in any integrated society, one must obviously consider how to deal with intermarried Jewish couples and their families. Tevye, the leading character in the production, "Fiddler on the Roof," addresses the intermarriage of one of his daughters by cutting her off from the family and treating her intermarriage as though she had died. Others, choose to do all they can to embrace what they consider to be Jewish families on the brink of being lost to our people forever. They hope that by extending kindness, concern, and warmth, these peripheral families might be brought back closer to the Jewish fold. Finally, it goes without saying, that there is an infinite number of responses in between these positions. In the past, different positions have meted out different results, and undoubtedly, each has its strengths and weaknesses.

Conservative Judaism is devoted to Jewish marriage, to Jewish children, and to Jewish families. While we are committed to encouraging marriage within the Jewish community, when intermarriage occurs, we must reach out to both the Jewish and non-Jewish spouse and both of their families. Rabbi Jerome M. Epstein, former CEO and Executive Vice President of the United Synagogue for Conservative Judaism addressed the issue of building Jewish families in his December 2005 address at the USCJ Biennial convention:

> "….Rejecting the intermarried family must not be our response. Welcoming and being open is a vital first step. Too often, we act as if being warm, welcoming, and supportive is our goal —that such behavior is sufficient to meet the challenge. It is not! Although attitudes of welcome and warmth are important and creating Jewish cultural and social connections should be applauded as vital first steps, these acts are hardly sufficient to guarantee Jewish survival. To achieve that end we must focus our outreach. Our goal must be to raise Jewish families.

> Studies have demonstrated that in 96 percent of the homes in which there are two Jewish parents the children are raised as Jews. In only one third of homes with one Jewish parent are children raised as Jews. The current intermarriage rate is 22 percent for children with two Jewish parents, but in households where only one parent is Jewish that rate is a staggering 74 percent. The challenge for Conservative Judaism, therefore, is to refocus our efforts and our energy.

> We must create Jewish families to ensure continuity and to create the Jewish renaissance of which we dream. But we also must inspire intermarried Jews to choose Judaism out of conviction that Jewish living will enrich their lives. Our outreach must reflect our values. We must become the movement that passionately encourages conversion and the raising of Jewish children…"

While there are many worthwhile responses to addressing the crisis of intermarriage, it would be incongruent with concern over the future of the Jewish people not to mention the terrible threat which this reality poses to our people. While there are those who intermarry and remain active or even become involved in Jewish life, this participation in Judaism has been statistically proven to be short-lived. Surveys have showed us that the children of intermarried families show a tendency to forgo active participation in Jewish life and even to revert some elements of other religions. This fact cannot be taken lightly when assessing the seriousness of this topic. Intermarriage, simply put, threatens the survival of the Jewish people.

What do you think synagogues should do to become more welcoming to people who are intermarried?

Commitments and Homosexuality

Same-sex marriage and other gay and lesbian issues have been actively discussed in the Conserva-tive Movement in recent years. In December 2006 the Law Committee of the Conservative Move-ment, which determines official positions of Conservative Judaism on matters of Jewish law, voted to accept two positions: one reaffirming the status quo in which the Conservative Movement does not authorize same-sex marriages, and one permitting Conservative rabbis to conduct same-sex commitment ceremonies. This position also permits the ordination of rabbis who are gay or lesbian. It remains to be seen whether and how Conservative rabbis and institutions will change their prac-tices based on the outcome of this vote. The Conservative Movement has endorsed civil rights for gay men and lesbians including inclusion in the synagogue community.

We will explore this further in Chapter Ten.

Chapter Ten
Physical Intimacy

How do you show care and support for dating partners?

A Kiss to Build A Dream On

There is magic in the simple kiss, although in today's world, it often is understated. In the Tanach, the word neshikah (kiss) appears 32 times in different forms.

For the most part, the kiss is a sign of familial love or a sign of cooperation and respect:

כז וַיִּגַּשׁ, וַיִּשַּׁק-לוֹ, וַיָּרַח אֶת-רֵיחַ בְּגָדָיו, וַיְבָרְכֵהוּ; וַיֹּאמֶר, רְאֵה רֵיחַ בְּנִי, כְּרֵיחַ שָׂדֶה, אֲשֶׁר בֵּרְכוֹ יְהוָה.

27 And he came near, and kissed him. And he smelled the smell of his raiment, and blessed him, and said: See, the smell of my son is as the smell of a field which the Lord has blessed.

(Bereishit 27:27)

יא וַיִּשַּׁק יַעֲקֹב, לְרָחֵל; וַיִּשָּׂא אֶת-קֹלוֹ, וַיֵּבְךְּ.

11 And Jacob kissed Rachel, and lifted up his voice, and wept

(Bereishit 29:11)

ב יִשָּׁקֵנִי מִנְּשִׁיקוֹת פִּיהוּ, כִּי-טוֹבִים דֹּדֶיךָ מִיָּיִן.

2 Kiss me from the kisses of your lips, for your love is more delightful than wine.

(Shir HaShirim 1:2)

Think of the point at which two infinites meet, the distant horizon where sky and earth touch. Edges blurred. Unclear where one begins and the other ends. This is the definition the kabbalists gave to the *even shtiyah*, the foundation stone which marked the connecting point between heaven and earth. This stone sat at the entrance to the Garden of Eden. It was the place where Abraham offered up Isaac. It is the heart of Mount Moriah. It is the place where *nashkei ar'a v'rakia ahad'dei*, where heaven and earth kiss. The point of ultimate connection.

The kiss. There in our very own tradition, that moment when two people become lost in one another. Where time stops and the world stands still. Breathtaking.
It's true, the tradition has much to say about sexuality. And those pages are meant to be turned, at the right and appropriate time. For right now, though, this kiss can be enough.

(Excerpted from The Month of Kiss-Lev by Rabbi Elyse Winick, Associate Director for Koach, United Synagogue of Conservative Judaism, November 2004.)

Choosing a Partner—What's Love Got to Do With It?

How do we get to the point in a relationship where we are ready for a kiss? When do we decide that we want to be more intimate or physical in a relationship? Can we only become intimate with those for whom we have loving feelings?

Let's take a look at a well-known text from the first line of the Shema:

ה וְאָהַבְתָּ, אֵת יְהֹוָה אֱלֹהֶיךָ, בְּכָל-לְבָבְךָ
וּבְכָל-נַפְשְׁךָ, וּבְכָל-מְאֹדֶךָ.

5 And you shall love the Lord your God with all of your heart, and with all of your soul, and with all of your might.

(D'varim 6:5)

- *What kind of love is this text talking about?*
- *Can you love God with the same intensity as you can have for another person?*
- *What does it mean to love someone with all of your heart, soul and might?*

What is Love?

How would you define love? Is it feelings? Actions? Words?
Why is love an important part of an intimate relationship?

Love is confusing. Love can sometimes be confused with feelings of lust or infatuation. Confusing these feelings can be harmful and lead to hurt and disappointment.

Are you in love, or just infatuated?

Unlike love, infatuation doesn't last. As soon as the 'going gets tough, it doesn't seem worth it to continue the relationship. When you're infatuated, you're more interested in what you can get out of the relationship than on what you can give to the relationship. It's really all about you. It's important to know the difference – because when you choose a partner for marrying or for a long-term relationship, you want to be sure you're in love, and not just in it for his cute looks! Lust fizzles and you soon "get over" feelings of infatuation. Love is everlasting.

Are there different kinds of love?

What is the difference between loving your parents or your siblings, your friends and loving a dating partner?

The different types of love- *Like and Love*

Let's take a look at a conversation between two characters in the 1999 movie, "10 Things I Hate About You":

> **Bianca:** There's a difference between like and love. Because, I like my Skechers, but I love my Prada backpack.
> **Chastity:** But I love my Skechers.
> **Bianca:** That's because you don't have a Prada backpack.

You likely found this funny. Why?

This is a scene from a Hollywood movie script. Does Bianca really understand what it means to "love?" How could you use the same words to describe how you feel about your new shoes that you use for your feelings toward your parents? Be careful, Hollywood movie scripts misguide us into false impressions of love, making it even more difficult to grasp.

כָּל אַהֲבָה שֶׁהִיא תְלוּיָה בְדָבָר, בָּטֵל דָּבָר, בְּטֵלָה אַהֲבָה. וְשֶׁאֵינָה תְּלוּיָה בְדָבָר, אֵינָה בְּטֵלָה לְעוֹלָם. אֵיזוֹ הִיא אַהֲבָה הַתְּלוּיָה בְדָבָר, זוֹ אַהֲבַת אַמְנוֹן וְתָמָר. וְשֶׁאֵינָה תְּלוּיָה בְדָבָר, זוֹ אַהֲבַת דָּוִיד וִיהוֹנָתָן:	Whenever love depends upon something and it passes, then the love passes away too. But if love does not depend upon some ulterior interest then the love will never pass away. What is an example of the love which depended upon some material advantage? That of Amnon for Tamar. And what is an example of the love which did not depend upon some ulterior interest? That of David and Jonathan.

(Pirkei Avot 5:18)

> **What are the different types of love that come to mind?**
>
> 1.
> 2.
> 3.
> 4.

Jewish philosophers make a distinction between *ahava she-hi te'luya b'davar*, conditional love, and *ahava she'ayno te'luya b'davar*, unconditional love.

> **What is the difference between conditional and unconditional love? Can you think of an example of each?**
>
> Conditional love is _____
>
> Unconditional love is _____

The Conditions of Love

As we see from the Pirkei Avot text on the previous page, there are different types of love. Your parents love you unconditionally, but your dating partner may not.

Can you think of any relationships (actual or fictional) where one of the partners was only in it to "get something" out of it or was taking advantage of the other for personal or material gain? Or a relationship where the love depended on something that didn't last such as wealth or beauty?

Do relationships that are conditional (i.e. she's with her partner because of wealth or status) last?

Is marriage conditional? If yes, does this mean that if it is based on the condition of wealth that it will dissolve if the couple becomes poor? If no, does this mean that even if one partner is unfaithful that the other will continue to love him/her nonetheless?

When do the rules of conditional/unconditional love become blurred?

- *Are these relationships happy, positive or secure? Could they be? Why or why not?*
- *What are the consequences to conditional love? How can we tell the difference so as to prevent suffering the pain and disappointment of conditional love?*

How can you apply this to your own life?
As a teenager, it may be tempting to enter into a relationship based on the condition of physical attraction. But what happens if (God forbid), one of you suffers burns from a fire or suffers an illness which alters your appearance. Suddenly, the love fizzles because it was *conditional.*

What happens when that something no longer exists?
Is conditional love a healthy kind of love?

Unconditional love happens when two people are deeply emotionally connected to each other.

Activity: Difficult to Define

What would you consider each of the following, conditional or unconditional?

_____Parent and child
_____Spouses
_____Common law relationship (live like a married couple but not legally bound)
_____Live-in relationship
_____Grandparent-grandchild

What are different ways people express love to each other? Think broadly about friendships and relationships in general.

People express love by:

When is it love?

How do you know when a relationship is based on love and not just sexual attraction? Think about yourself and your partner. See if your primary concern is, "What's in it for me?" or, "Are my needs being met?" Do you say to your partner, "If you loved me, you'd let me." This describes a situation where your primary concern is your gratification. It is obvious that you primary motivation is your personal desires and sexuality rather than love for the other person.

Many people say that love takes over from sexuality when you care more about the other person than you care about yourself —when you begin to say, "What can I do to make the other person happy?" "What can I do to provide happiness, fulfillment, and need satisfaction for my partner? Now this makes sense up to a point. It fits with our romantic understanding of what love is. It fits with our sometimes unreal situation. It does have the advantage of moving out of selfishness and concern with one's own sexuality and personal gratification, but it has the disadvantage of being unrealistic. It's unfair to expect that any one person can so minimize his or her own desire to have personal needs satisfied and concentrate solely on gratifying somebody else's needs. In the average person, that sets up unreal expectations and almost guarantees and invite failure. One of the major troubles with relationships and marriages today is that people have set up totally unrealistic expectations, either from the perspective of satisfying personal needs or from the perspective of satisfying the other person's needs. Since both of these perspectives represent a certain amount of immaturity, it is no wonder that so many relationships fail.

A more mature way of looking at love is that there is "you" and there is "your partner." Each of you is an individual with personal needs, desires, and sexuality; together you have created a new entity, "the two of us." The emphasis is on the relationship. The emphasis is on maintaining and developing the relationship, and meeting the needs of this new entity that you have created, the entity known as "we." It's not, "How can I make you happier?" but, "How can we make ourselves happier?" It's not, "What are my needs and how can they be filled?" but, "What are our needs and how can we work together to fill them?" At this level, love is dominant and stress can be tolerated. Challenges, crises, or conflicts become an opportunity for mutual problem-solving, leading to an even stronger relationship.

It is important to remember, however, that the "we" is still made up of "you" and "me." Simply creating this positive unit known as "we" or "us" does not mean that you and I completely lose our individuality. There are really three entities: "you," with all your needs and desires, "me," with mine; and "us." The fact that we are part of the "us" means that we give up a certain amount of individuality in order to contribute to the joint entity, but cannot completely deny the necessity to be ourselves at the same times as we contribute to the life, health, and happiness of the collective "we."

Being human – and, therefore, capable of being influenced by yetzer ha-ra (the evil inclination) and yetzer tov (good inclination), we sometimes move among these three different levels. What matters is the level at which we spend most of our time, always trying to fulfill our goal.

Before we consider our own approaches to sexuality, here are three biblical excerpts dealing with love, marriage, and sexual attraction. **Examine the biblical passages quoted in light of what has been said about love and sexual attraction.**

Isaac and Rebekah

סג וַיֵּצֵא יִצְחָק לָשׂוּחַ בַּשָּׂדֶה, לִפְנוֹת עָרֶב; וַיִּשָּׂא עֵינָיו וַיַּרְא, וְהִנֵּה גְמַלִּים בָּאִים.

63 And Isaac went out to meditate in the field at the eventide; and he lifted up his eyes, and saw, and, there were camels coming.

סד וַתִּשָּׂא רִבְקָה אֶת-עֵינֶיהָ, וַתֵּרֶא אֶת-יִצְחָק; וַתִּפֹּל, מֵעַל הַגָּמָל.

64 And Rebekah lifted up her eyes, and when she saw Isaac, she alighted from the camel.

סה וַתֹּאמֶר אֶל-הָעֶבֶד, מִי-הָאִישׁ הַלָּזֶה הַהֹלֵךְ בַּשָּׂדֶה לִקְרָאתֵנוּ, וַיֹּאמֶר הָעֶבֶד, הוּא אֲדֹנִי; וַתִּקַּח הַצָּעִיף, וַתִּתְכָּס.

65 And she said unto the servant: 'What man is this that walks in the field to meet us?' And the servant said: 'It is my master.' And she took her veil, and covered herself.

סו וַיְסַפֵּר הָעֶבֶד, לְיִצְחָק, אֵת כָּל-הַדְּבָרִים, אֲשֶׁר עָשָׂה.

66 And the servant told Isaac all the things that he had done.

סז וַיְבִאֶהָ יִצְחָק, הָאֹהֱלָה שָׂרָה אִמּוֹ, וַיִּקַּח אֶת-רִבְקָה וַתְּהִי-לוֹ לְאִשָּׁה, וַיֶּאֱהָבֶהָ; וַיִּנָּחֵם יִצְחָק, אַחֲרֵי אִמּוֹ.

67 And Isaac brought her into his mother Sarah's tent, and took Rebekah, and she became his wife; and he loved her. And Isaac was comforted after his mother's death.

(Bereishit 24:63-67)

Jacob, Leah and Rachel

טז וּלְלָבָן, שְׁתֵּי בָנוֹת: שֵׁם הַגְּדֹלָה לֵאָה, וְשֵׁם הַקְּטַנָּה רָחֵל.

16 Now Laban had two daughters: the name of the elder was Leah, and the name of the younger was Rachel.

יז וְעֵינֵי לֵאָה, רַכּוֹת; וְרָחֵל, הָיְתָה, יְפַת-תֹּאַר, וִיפַת מַרְאֶה.

17 And Leah's eyes were weak; but Rachel was of beautiful form and fair to look upon.

יח וַיֶּאֱהַב יַעֲקֹב, אֶת-רָחֵל; וַיֹּאמֶר, אֶעֱבָדְךָ שֶׁבַע שָׁנִים, בְּרָחֵל בִּתְּךָ, הַקְּטַנָּה.

18 And Jacob loved Rachel; and he said: 'I will serve thee seven years for Rachel thy younger daughter.'

יט וַיֹּאמֶר לָבָן, טוֹב תִּתִּי אֹתָהּ לָךְ, מִתִּתִּי אֹתָהּ, לְאִישׁ אַחֵר; שְׁבָה, עִמָּדִי.

19 And Laban said: 'It is better that I give her to you, than that I should give her to another man; stay with me.'

כ וַיַּעֲבֹד יַעֲקֹב בְּרָחֵל, שֶׁבַע שָׁנִים; וַיִּהְיוּ בְעֵינָיו כְּיָמִים אֲחָדִים, בְּאַהֲבָתוֹ אֹתָהּ.

20 And Jacob served seven years for Rachel; and they seemed unto him but a few days, for the love he had to her.

כא וַיֹּאמֶר יַעֲקֹב אֶל-לָבָן הָבָה אֶת-אִשְׁתִּי, כִּי מָלְאוּ יָמָי; וְאָבוֹאָה, אֵלֶיהָ.

21 And Jacob said unto Laban: 'Give me my wife, for my days are filled, that I may go in to her.'

(Bereishit 29:16-21)

David and Batsheva

Late one afternoon, David rose from his couch and strolled on the roof of the royal palace; and from the roof he saw a woman bathing. The woman was very beautiful, and the king sent someone to make inquiries about the woman. He reported, "She is Batsheva daughter of Eliam (and) wife of Uriah the Hittitie." David sent messengers to fetch her; she came to him and he lay with her- she had just purified herself after her period— and she went back home. The woman conceived, and she sent word to David, "I am pregnant." Thereupon David sent a message to Joab, "Send Uriah the Hittite to me," and Joab sent Uriah to David.

When Uriah came to him, David asked him how Joab and the troops were faring and how the journey was. Then David said to Uriah, "Go down to your house and bathe your feet." When Uriah left the royal palace, a present from the king followed him. But Uriah slept at the entrance of the royal palace, along with the other officers of his lord, and did not go down to his house. When David was told that Uriah had not gone down to his house, he said to Uriah, "You just came from a journey, why didn't you go down to your house?" Uriah answered David, "The Ark and Israel and Judah are located at Succot, and my master Joab and Your Majesty's men are camped in the open; how can I go home and eat and drink and sleep with my wife? As you live, by your very life, I will not do this!" David said to Urah, "Stay here today also, and tomorrow I will send you off." So Uriah remained in Jerusalem that day. The next day, David summoned him, and he ate and drank with him until he got him drunk; but in the evening, (Uriah) went out to sleep in the same place, with his Lord's officers; he did not go down to his home.

In the morning, David wrote a letter to Joab, which he sent with Uriah. He wrote in the letter as follows: "Place Uriah in the frontline where the fighting is fiercest; then fall back so that he may be killed." So when Joab was besieging the city, he stationed Uriah at the point where he knew that there were able warriors. The men of the city attacked Joab, and some of David's officers among the troops fell; Uriah the Hittite was among those who died.

When Uriah's wife, Batsheva, heard that her husband Uriah was dead, she lamented over her husband. After the period of mourning was over, David sent and had her brought into his palace; she became his wife and bore him a son. ... The Lord afflicted the child that Uriah's wife had borne to David, and it became critically ill. David entreated God for the boy.

David fasted, and he went in and spent the night lying on the ground. The senior servants of his household tried to induce him to get up from the ground; but he refused, nor would he partake of food with them. On the seventh day the child died. Thereupon David rose from the ground; he bathed and anointed himself, and he changed his clothes. He went into the House of the Lord and prostrated himself.

David consoled his wife Batsheva; he went to her and lay with her. She bore a son and she named him Solomon. The Lord favored him, and He sent a message through the prophet Nathan; and he was named Yedidyah at the instance of the Lord.

(II Shmuel 11:2-17, 26-27; 12:15-18, 20, 24-25)

For Further Thought:

- *Can you find examples of romantic love? selfish love? mature love?*

- *Can you find examples of sexual attraction being primary? Or of concern for the joint relationship being stronger than the desire of either partner?*

- *Look at the sequence of events in the relationship between Isaac and Rebekah. How would that sequence be written if it were being done in Hollywood or in a modern novel? Explain or comment on the differences that you could imagine.*

- *What can you defer from the text about the relationships between Jacob and Leah, and between Jacob and Rachel. Was one relationship superficial? Was one deeper?*

- *Think of a couple that you know who get along very well with each other. They could be people your own age; your parents, relatives, or friends; married or unmarried. Now think of a couple you know who appear not to have a very good relationship. Again, they may be married or unmarried; your age or any age; relatives or friends.*

- *What are some of the behaviors that each couple exhibits that give you the clue that they are getting along or not getting along? Is there a pattern to these behaviors that you are able to identify? To what extent are the relationships characterized by selfishness, immaturity, self-denial, idolization of the partner, or a willingness to work things out together?*

Kedusha in Intimate Relationships

An expression of love is the physical interaction or intimacy between partners. Intimate relationships (those in committed relationships), are filled with instances of *kedusha*, holiness.

Which relationship is more *kadosh*—one between a person and God, or a person and a partner? Think back to our discussion about the categories of mitzvot in the first chapter.

As in all other aspects of our lives, Judaism helps guide us toward a moral and ethical approach to sexual interaction. The Jewish perspective on sex is important because "religion depicts the ways we are linked to each other, to the environment, to God." Sex is not just a physical activity but a holy expression of the deepest form of intimacy between human beings.

> When sex [within marriage] is done for the sake of Heaven, there is nothing so holy and pure.
>
> Rambam

In the same way that we elevate our relationships to a level of *kedusha* by ensuring they are healthy and founded in love and respect, we also elevate sexual behavior to a level of *kedusha*.

In other religions such as Catholicism, the supreme relationship is between a person and God: Monks practice asceticism, where they separate themselves from the general public and live a life of abstinence and severity, and priests and nuns abstain from sex and other worldly enjoyments, in order to bring themselves closer to God.

> Maimonides, known, after the initial letters of his name (**R**abbi **M**oshe **B**en **M**aimon, "Rabbi Moses son of Maimon") as Rambam, is generally acknowledged to be the greatest Jewish thinker, Talmudist, and codifier in the Middle Ages. He lived in the 12th century in Spain.

In Judaism, however, the pinnacle of relationships is one between two people—in this case, between two people who have made a lifetime commitment to each other (or in the early stages, between two dating partners). Think back to our discussion about one of the names of God—HaMakom. God's presence rests with us not when we separate ourselves from others, but when we work on our interactions with others, and when we elevate our relationships to a level of kedusha.

There are many steps to a Jewish marriage ceremony, the first of which is called kiddushin, which has the Hebrew root kadosh. Traditional marriage laws require a man to say to the woman "*haray at mekudeshet li*". Again, we see the root word *kadosh* here—although this is commonly translated as "Behold, you are betrothed to me," if we translate this phrase literally, it means "Behold, you are made holy to me." Today, many couples choose to say this to each other.

How do we elevate our relationships to a level of *kedusha*?

Activity: The Ladder of Kedusha:

Consider the question above about the levels of holiness. Place the following relationships on the ladder of Kedusha depending on how you view the holiness of each relationship.

God and person

Person and self

Person and friend

Person and parent

Person and sibling

Person and dating partner

Person and spouse

Just as we respect the holiness in our selves, we must also respect the holiness in each other. A *kadosh* relationship is one in which both partners love, trust and respect each other. This is the strongest foundation on which two people can build a relationship.

Sex, Love, and Rock and Roll

We want to make it clear that one of the purposes of this section is to give you the tools, from a Jewish perspective to make informed, mature decisions. As Judaism can guide you through all other actions and decisions in your life, sex, likely one of the most prominent issues in your life, should also be looked at through a Jewish lens.

Sexual relations are a vital part of Jewish life, and necessary for ensuring the survival of the Jewish people. In fact, having sexual relations is the first commandment given in the Torah:

כח וַיְבָרֶךְ אֹתָם, אֱלֹהִים, וַיֹּאמֶר לָהֶם אֱלֹהִים פְּרוּ וּרְבוּ וּמִלְאוּ אֶת-הָאָרֶץ

28 God blessed them and said to them: "Be fruitful and multiply and fill the earth."

(Bereishit 1:28)

But like everything else in Judaism, we have laws about how to engage in sexual activity and we must remember that this is reserved for people who are married to each other.

א וְהָאָדָם, יָדַע אֶת-חַוָּה אִשְׁתּוֹ; וַתַּהַר, וַתֵּלֶד אֶת-קַיִן, וַתֹּאמֶר, קָנִיתִי אִישׁ אֶת-יְהוָה.

1 Now Adam knew his wife Eve, and she conceived and gave birth to Cain.

(Bereishit 4:1)

The text uses the word *yadah*, to know, to describe the sexual relationship between Adam and Eve. **What can we learn from this?**

ג וַתִּקַּח שָׂרַי אֵשֶׁת-אַבְרָם, אֶת-הָגָר הַמִּצְרִית שִׁפְחָתָהּ, מִקֵּץ עֶשֶׂר שָׁנִים, לְשֶׁבֶת אַבְרָם בְּאֶרֶץ כְּנָעַן; וַתִּתֵּן אֹתָהּ לְאַבְרָם אִישָׁהּ, לוֹ לְאִשָּׁה.

3 And Sarai, Abram's wife, took Hagar the Egyptian, her handmaid, after Abram had dwelled ten years in the land of Canaan, and gave her to Abram her husband to be his wife.

ד וַיָּבֹא אֶל-הָגָר, וַתַּהַר; וַתֵּרֶא כִּי הָרָתָה, וַתֵּקַל גְּבִרְתָּהּ בְּעֵינֶיהָ.

4 And he went in unto Hagar, and she conceived; and when she saw that she had conceived, her mistress was despised in her eyes.

(Bereishit 16:3-4)

What about Hagar – how do you think she felt about Abraham's action? How does using the word *yavo* (literally "to come (here translated as "cohabited")) make Abraham's behavior different than Adam's?

Activity: True or False

_____ A sexual partner should be someone you love
_____ Love leads to sex
_____ You can't have sex without emotional attachment
_____ You don't have to love the person you have sex with
_____ Hooking up is no big deal, everyone does it
_____ Sex is just an act, there isn't anything emotional about it
_____ You don't have to respect the person you have sex with
_____ Oral sex isn't sex
_____ Sex leads to love

Share your answers from this activity with a friend. Do you agree or disagree on any statements?

What is the relationship between sex and love?

Does an intimate relationship have to include sex? If there is no sex, does that mean the partners do not love each other?

Rabbi Dorff explains that, within a marriage, sexual relations bring people closer to God by fulfilling the divine purposes of companionship *and* procreation:

> "The Torah thus recognizes the basic human need for intimate companionship and seeks to satisfy that need through the institution of marriage," writes Rabbi Dorff in his Rabbinic Letter. "Sex is one of the ways in which this companionship is expressed. The Torah recognized the sexual desires of women as well as those of men; while we might take that for granted, other societies in the ancient – and, for that matter, in the medieval and the modern— world assumed that only men have sexual appetites. Instead the Torah and the Rabbis who later interpret it, in recognition of the couple's mutual desires, structure the laws of marriage such that both spouses have rights to sex with regularity within marriage..."
> (Dorff, This Is My Beloved, page 14)

In addition to being a way to experience pleasure and wholeness, sex is a way to experience holiness. While one of the purposes of sexual relations is of course to have children (the first commandment after all is "be fruitful and multiply") it is not the only reason. It may surprise you to learn that we are in fact commanded in the Torah to have sexual relations with our spouse, as a source of pleasure.

In Judaism, both the wife and the husband have a right to relations with each other and most importantly, the sexual activity may not be coerced by either one. Both partners must consent and desire each other. This is in line with the idea that holiness exists when there are sexual relations between a wife and husband, two intimate and committed partners who trust and love each other.

Let's look back at Catholicism again. Priests and nuns abstain from sexual behavior because it is considered a "base desire." Judaism does not necessarily disagree—there are many rules and regulations governing sexual behavior. But instead of asking us to abstain from it, Judaism teaches how to take this human need and elevate it to a level of *kedusha*.

Right Time, Right Place, Right Person

In Judaism, sex is permitted—even required—within the context of marriage. Casual and promiscuous sexual encounters are condemned because they do not involve love or commitment.

> One should know that sexual union is holy and pure when it is done as it should be, at the time it should be, and with the proper intent. We the possessors of the Torah believe that God created all, and did not create anything ugly or shameful. For if sexual intercourse were repulsive... than all of God's creations are also repulsive.
>
> Rabbi Moses ben Nahman, (Nahmanides)
> Iggeret Ha-Kodesh (The Holy Letter)

Rabbi Moshe ben Nahman (Nahmanides) was a Spanish Talmudist, Kabbalist, and biblical exegete (1194-1270), known, after the initial letters of his name, as Ramban. He rebutted Maimonides' opinion that marriage was only for procreation and only to be done when necessary, with his letter **"Igeret Hakodesh."** In this document, he relies on his medical and mystical knowledge to discuss the holiness of the marital union.

How can one determine when and what "it should be" and what exactly is "the proper intent?" Your mind is probably plagued by the same questions when you are faced with making decisions about sexual intimacy. How do you know what is right for you?

Sex should be more than just a physical or biological act. Sex is ideally about connecting with someone on a deeply emotional level. Rather than being the basis for a relationship, sex should be the culmination of a relationship in which two people are committed to each other, and love and respect each other:

> No one should claim that it (intercourse) is ugly or unseemly. God forbid! For intercourse is called "knowing" and not in vain is it called thus... We who have the Torah and believe that God created all in his wisdom [do not believe that God] created anything inherently ugly or unseemly. If we were to say that intercourse is repulsive, then we blaspheme God who made the genitals...Whatever ugliness is there, comes from how a person uses them. All organs of the body are neutral; the use made of them determines whether they are holy or unholy... (Birth Control in Jewish Law, David Feldman, 1968, p. 99)

Unlike in other faiths where sex may be regarded as ugly or sinful, Judaism views sex as a beautiful and loving act.

Rabbi Dorff explains the Jewish perspective on sex within the confines of marriage:

Activity: Holding hands, kisses, budding romance...

Rabbi Dorff explains the Jewish perspective on sex within the confines of marriage. Read the following excerpts from Rabbi Dorff's rabbinical letter and choose which one(s) you agree with, disagree with or helps you formulate your own opinion:

"The Torah recognizes the basic human need for intimate companionship and seeks to satisfy that need through the institution of marriage."

"After Adam experienced the pain of aloneness, only then would he be ready to appreciate the need for companionship and interdependence as the essential path of personal fulfillment. For him and for us, his descendants, this is the human norm. Sex is one of the ways in which this companionship is expressed."

"Marriage is the most profound relationship we enter and therefore one of the most demanding undertakings. It touches our deepest human longings for love, trust and intimacy and therefore brings out the very best and the very worst of who we are as individuals"

"Only marriages can attain the holiness and communal sanction of *Kiddushin* [the first stage of marriage, the betrothal between two people where the commitment to one another, including sexual union is accepted], because it is the marital context which holds out the most promise that people can live by those views and values in their intimate relationships. Judaism would therefore have us refrain from sexual intercourse outside marriage"

"Why does Judaism posit marriage as the appropriate context for sexual intercourse? It does so because in that setting the couple can attain the threefold purpose of marital sex... namely, **companionship, procreation and the education of the next generation**. While non-marital sex can provide companionship as well as physical release, especially in the context of a long-term relationship, unmarried couples generally do not take the responsibilities of having and educating children. They may care deeply for each other, especially in a long-term relationship, but their unwillingness to get married usually signifies that they are not ready to make a lifetime commitment."

Rabbi Dorff draws on the following basic Jewish values to form the Conservative perspective on sexual intimacy, some of which have been previously discussed in this book:

- B'tzelem Elohim—being created in the image of God—"we are privileged to commune with God and in rabbinic terms, even to be God's partner in ongoing acts of creation."

- Tzniut/Modesty—the privacy of sex—sex is a private act and should be kept private— "while sex in Judaism is not a corrupting or embarrassing part of our existence... Jewish Law does require that it be held private....This enables sexual intercourse more effectively to bind the couple together emotionally, for this is an aspect of their lives that they share together in private... Jewish rules mandating privacy in sexual matters also help to limit sexual intercourse to the context of marriage, where Jewish sources declare that it belongs."

- Respect for others/K'vod Habriot—"In every relationship, one must treat other human beings with the respect worthy of a creature of God…this means minimally, that sexual relations, if they are to adhere to Jewish concepts and values, must not be coercive."

- Honesty—"Judaism demands of us a high standard of honesty, for respect for other human begins entails that we do not deceive them…the Rabbis require that "one's 'yes' should be yes and one's 'no' should be no."

- Love and fidelity—ve'ahavta l'rayecha kamocha: if we are to support our friends, the support we show a romantic partner should be even stronger. "This means that in such relationships, we must care for our partner in both feeling and action. Negatively, we may not offend or annoy him or her, take him or her for granted and certainly not harm him or her in any way. Positively, love requires that we think of the other's needs and wants in living our own lives and that we make a point of attending to them."

- Health and Safety—"Contrary to the contemporary notion that my body belongs to me, our tradition teaches us that our bodies belong to God. As owner, God can and does demand that we take care of our bodies throughout our lives, very much like the owner of an apartment requiring that those who rent it take reasonable care of it during its occupancy. Jewish Law therefore prescribes a number of positive obligations that we have to take care of our bodies (proper sleep, exercise, diet and hygiene) and it forbids mutilation of the body, taking undue risks with it and suicide."

- Holiness—Judaism demands of us that we live by the highest of moral standards, that we emulate God [Vayikra 19:2- "You shall be holy; for I the Lord your God am holy."]… Sex is one important area where this aspiration [to be holy] must be manifest…sex as understood in the Jewish tradition can distance one from God if one violates some of Judaism's norms relevant to it, but sex can also bring human lives closer to God, as one fulfills the divine purpose of companionship and procreation. In fact, probably the most famous rabbinic letter on sexual morality in the Middle Ages, that attributed to Rabbi Moses ben Nahman (Nahmanides) is entitled **The Letter of Holiness/Igeret Hakodesh**, and the section of Rabbi Abraham ben David of Posquiere's book on family law dealing with moral and theological prisms through which one should approach sexual activity is called *Sha'ar Ha-Kedusha*: the Gate of Holiness. **Thus, sex in the Jewish tradition can be a vehicle not only for pleasure, celebration and wholeness, but also for holiness.**

Teenagers and Sex

Sex is an important part of a marital relationship. While Judaism fully understands that teenagers may want to have sex, it does not condone sex for teens. It is very important for teens to meet each other, have fun together, and feel comfortable in each other's presence. It also allows teens who are forming romantic relationships to hold hands, hug, and kiss each other, as long as this is voluntary behavior for both and done in a private manner. Rabbi Dorff continues his message to teenagers:

Even more than single adults, though, teenagers need to refrain from sexual intercourse, for they cannot honestly deal with its implications or results— including the commitments and responsibilities that sexual relations normally imply, the possibility of children, and the risk of AIDS and other sexually transmitted diseases. Abstinence is surely not easy when the physical and social pressures are strong, but it is the only responsible thing to do. (Dorff, 36)

Non-marital sex

What about sexual relations between consenting adults in a loving, committed relationship?

Sex is ideally reserved for married couples. However, we live in a modern world where sex between consenting adults in a loving committed relationship is common. We know that there are situations where non-married committed couples decide to have sex. What does Rabbi Dorff say about that and what do you think?

> "Judaism posits marriage as the appropriate context for sexual intercourse. We recognize though, that many Jews are engaging in sexual relations outside the marital bond... We also condemn casual and promiscuous sexual encounters since they involve little or no love or commitment...." (Dorff, page 30)

Not all acts of intimacy are discouraged outside of marriage. Touching is natural and an expression of love:

> Romantic relationships from their earliest stages and throughout their unfolding often use these forms of affection too. Holding hands, hugging and kissing are perfectly natural and healthy expressions of both a budding romance and a long term one. One must take due regard for the sense of **modesty and privacy** which Judaism would have us preserve in expressing our romantic feelings, and so the more intense forms of these activities should be reserved for private quarters." (Dorff, page 30)

Which values from the original list does this excerpt reflect?

> "Some people though, **either will not or cannot get married** and the physical and psychological pleasures which sex provides leads them to engage in sexual relationships with each other. **Judaism cannot condone such relationships. Nevertheless, for those Jews who do engage in them, all of the concepts described [above] apply to their sexual activities... in fact, in the context of non-marital relationships, some of [what was outlined above] take on new significance."**

Before we continue, look at the list from earlier in the chapter and decide how some of these values could also be applied to relations between non-married partners:

Btzelem Elohim
Kavod/Respect
Tzniut/Modesty
Honesty
Fidelity
Health and Safety

Now read how Rabbi Dorff applies the significance of these values to sexual intimacy between non-married partners.

- B'tzelem Elohim—Seeing oneself and one's partner as the creatures of God: to paraphrase and reiterate—we are wholes created in the Image of God. Both partners are to be treated with the utmost respect. "Our sexual activity must reflect our value system and the personhood of the other. If it is only for physical pleasure, it degrades us terribly... it is all the more imperative in non-marital sex, where the lack of a public, long term commitment to one another only heightens the chances that one or both of the partners will see sex as simply pleasurable release."

- Respect for Others/K'vod Habriot—non coercive sex—"Unmarried people must take special care [to ensure respectful, non-coercive sex] because they know each other less well and are therefore more likely to misunderstand each other's cues.

- Tzniut—Modesty—"For singles, it is especially important to note that modesty requires that one's sexual activities be conducted in private and that they be not discussed with others."

- Honesty—"If one is not married, however, sex cannot possibly symbolize the same degree of commitment. Unmarried sexual partners must therefore openly and honestly confront what their sexual activity means for the length and depth of their relationship.

- Fidelity—Marriage by its very nature demands fidelity; unmarried relationships by their very nature do not... in the spirit of [fidelity], one should avoid short-term sexual encounters and seek instead, long-term relationships to which one remains faithful for the duration of the relationship.

- Health and Safety—"The concern of the Jewish tradition is even more critical in non-marital relationships than it is in married ones, for most sexually transmitted diseases are contracted in non-marital sexual liaisons."

In one or two sentences, according to Rabbi Dorff, sex within Judaism can be defined as:

_____

_____

_____

Each of us will interpret Rabbi Dorff's letter differently. The bottom line is that the sex dilemma is ultimately up to you. As in all other aspects of your life, Jewish values can help guide your decisions and sex is no exception. If you are able to apply the values outlined by Rabbi Dorff in your decision making, you will ultimately be making a Jewish decision, rooted in love, respect and holiness.

Over the next few chapters, we will talk about many issues related to friendships and to dating relationships, including: respect, equality, communication, sexual relations, conflict, relational aggression, and abuse. Remember, when you are reading various texts, that there was no such thing as "dating" in biblical times. This does not mean that what we learn here will not be applicable; it just means you will need to think about these in the larger scheme of "relationships."

- *Do you think that there are many pressures to have sex?*
- *When do you think it is appropriate to have sex?*
- *How would you decide whether to have sex or not?*
- *What would you tell the other person if you didn't want to have sex?*

Scenario 1:

Michael and Melanie are both juniors. They met last year and have been going out since then. Both are virgins but Melanie wants to 'seal the deal' and have sex; Michael doesn't want to have sex and doesn't know now whether that's because he'd just rather wait until he is older or if its because he is unsure about his feelings for Melanie. He feels pressure from Melanie and doesn't want to break up with her, but is concerned that if he doesn't give in, he'll lose her.

How can Michael share how he feels without looking and feeling like a 'wimp?'
What are some ways that Melanie might react?
What do you think they should do?

Scenario 2:

Jackie, Jason, Adam and Mara are hanging out on a Saturday night. The four of them are really close, but recently, Jackie and Jason have become closer and are now an "item." It's "Scary Movie" night at Jackie's and as soon as the lights dim, Jackie and Jason begin making out, leaving Mara and Adam feeling very uncomfortable with their public display of affection. Adam repeatedly pretends to cough and clear his throat and makes sarcastic comments to "get a room," hinting that they are increasingly uncomfortable with the action going on off-screen.

What should Adam and Mara do? Should they have to leave to give Jackie and Jason privacy?
How can they respectfully put an end to the Public Display of Affection (PDA)?
How would you feel if you were the other two? Would this make you uncomfortable?
Are Jackie and Jason being respectful? Are they considering the Jewish values of *Tzniut* or *Kavod*?

Scenario 3:

You are hanging out after school with two friends, Ben and Danny. Ben tells Danny that he has a crush on Melissa, another friend of yours. Danny tells Ben: "You should totally tap that, she's hot."

How do terms like "hooking up" and "tap that" impact the kedusha?
Does "hooking up" casually impact the way you see yourself?

- *What happens in each of these scenarios?*
- *What kind of status associated with engaging in sexual activity?*
- *How can it impact the way others see you?*

Scenario 4:

Jake is a senior in high school and is a 'player.' He asks Jenny, a junior, if she'd like to go with him to hear (name your favorite group). Jenny is flattered to be asked by Jake and agrees to go out with him. Jake buys two tickets for $150.00 each. He had earned the money for this date over the past month by mowing lawns. Jake picks Jen up at her house and the two of them go to the concert where they have a great time. After the concert, Jake asks Jenny if she'd like to stop by a party on their way home. The cover charge for the party is $10.00 which Jake pays. While they're walking into the party, Jake puts his arm around Jenny. While they're dancing, he leans in close and suggestively. They kiss a little bit and at midnight, the two of them leave. Rather than take Jenny directly home, as she is expecting, Jake pulls into a dark wooded area nearby. Jenny asks him what he is doing and Jake says he is pulling into there so they can 'have a good time.' Jenny protests – she wants to go home. Jake says to her: what do you mean? You went out with me, I spent a ton of money on you, you kissed me, and now I want to have sex with you. You owe it to me."

Does Jenny owe Jake sex?
Is Jake right or wrong to expect sex after spending money on the date?
Would the responses be different if they had split the cost of the date?
What about if they had been going out for a while?
Imagine if the figures were reversed – would the outcome be different if Jenny had asked Jake out?

- *Do you and your friends feel pressure to engage in sexual activity? Why or why not?*
- *Where does the pressure come from?*
- *How can teens deal with those pressures?*

Activity: Sex in the Media and Pop Culture

Consider the previous discussion on the media's influence. Where does sex fit in?

Try and recall the last popular magazine you flipped through and take a look at the ads.

Do the ads use sex or sexual innuendo/subliminal messaging to sell products?
Could the ads have sold the products in another way? Why does the marketing field use sexuality to sell their products? How does "sex sell"? What are the consequences to selling sexuality? How do the media downplay or remove kedusha from physical intimacy?
Do you think people are more likely to buy the product when it is advertised with sexual innuendo or without? Why?

What about television? Think of some reality shows you know with highly charged sexual characters – is that what makes them popular? Do you think that watching these shows, or others like them, have any impact on how you view what is and what is not appropriate or normal?

Name That Tune

Think about some of the music that is on your portable music player. What are most of the songs about? How many of them also have versions that are not played on the radio because the lyrics are inappropriate?

Some research found that teens who listen to music that contains sexually explicit lyrics or watch TV or movies with sex or sexual innuendo are likely to engage in sex earlier than teens who don't listen to or watch them?

Do you think this research is accurate? Why or why not?
How does listening to such music and/or watching such television, videos, movies, affect your own ideas about sex?

Intimacy Between Same Sex Couples

There are many influences that contribute to your personal attitudes about sex but when and with whom you engage in sexual activity is ultimately up to you. As long as you regard the person, yourself and the acts involved with *Kedusha*, you will be responding to these influences with the dignity, respect and holiness it deserves. The same is true with same-sex couples and intimacy between them however, perspectives differ on acceptance and openness.

As recently as 2006, the issue of same-sex intimacy has been discussed among members of the Committee on Jewish Law and Standards of the Conservative Movement (CJLS), which determines changes to principles and practices of Conservative Judaism rooted in Halachic argument. In Conservative Judaism, the CJLS will often set out more than one acceptable position.

The topic of homosexuality can be controversial within Judaism primarily because of the text from Vayikra prohibiting a male to have relations with a man in a manner which is similar to those he would have with a woman:

כב וְאֶת-זָכָר—לֹא תִשְׁכַּב, מִשְׁכְּבֵי
אִשָּׁה: תּוֹעֵבָה, הוּא.

22 And you should not lie with a man as you would with a woman; it is an abomination.
(Vayikra 18:22)

Although the Torah seems to forbid homosexual activity, contemporary Jewish thinkers engage in heated debate over the stricture and its applicability to today's world.

What do you think are the uniquely Jewish issues in the debate about same-sex commitments, sex and marriage?

Below, two perspectives are presented through summaries of *tshuvot* or Rabbinic responsa on sexual intimacy between same-sex partners from a Conservative Jewish perspective.

One opinion affirming same sex commitment ceremonies was authored by Rabbis Elliot Dorff, Daniel Nevins and Avram Reisner. This opinion received 13 votes in favor. (Six votes are needed for a t'shuva to become an acceptable practice.) According to the accepted *t'shuvah*, whereas in the past homosexuality had been considered abnormal and a mental illness, contemporary theories accept that sexual orientation is not a voluntary choice. Ensuring respect and dignity for all human beings is a central tenet of Judaism, and in fact, doing so supersedes both positive and negative *mitzvot*. Prohibiting homosexuality goes against this idea of *kivod habriyot* (respect for living things), marginalizing those who are attracted to a member of the same sex.

The responsum's legal findings were that:
1. The explicit biblical ban on anal sex between men remains in effect. Gay men are instructed to refrain from anal sex.
2. Heterosexual marriage between two Jews remains the halachic ideal. For homosexuals who are incapable of maintaining a heterosexual relationship, the rabbinic prohibitions that have been associated with other gay and lesbian intimate acts are superseded based upon the Talmudic principle of kevod habriot, our obligation to preserve the human dignity of all people.
3. The 1992 CJLS policy of welcoming homosexuals into congregations was extended and gay or lesbian Jews are to be welcomed into congregations as full members with no restrictions. In addition, gay and lesbian Jews should be welcomed into professional schools and associations.
4. This T'shuva did not rule on the halachic status of gay and lesbian relationships. It would require a new institution to deal with the ceremonies and legal instruments appropriate for creating homosexual unions, but also the norms for the dissolution of those couples. The responsum does not provide for *kiddushin* (marriage) for same-sex couples.

The responsum states that "stable, committed, Jewish relationships [are] as necessary and beneficial for homosexuals and their families as they are for heterosexuals," and prohibiting homosexuality would force someone to be alone for their entire life. While the actual prohibition described in the Torah does in fact remain, that is the only ban on sexual behavior for those in a same-sex relationship.

Rabbi Joel Roth held a different opinion which also received 13 votes in favor. Rabbi Roth felt that the 1992 CJLS policy of welcoming homosexuals into synagogues but not granting equal status in the synagogue should not be changed. Rabbi Roth maintained that "What is forbidden is sexual behavior with a partner with whom one could not legally have intercourse...." Rabbi Roth addresses the issue of lesbianism by saying that "The primary difference between male and female homosexuality is that one is biblically forbidden and the other is forbidden by the rabbis. Female homosexuality is no less forbidden by the law than by male homosexuality." He addressed the issue of kavod habriyot mentioned by Rabbis Dorff, Nevins and Reisner but concluded that the argument didn't apply to this. Ultimately, the legal decision:
1. Welcomed gays and lesbians into congregations, youth groups, camps and schools
2. Allows for homosexuals to have honors within worship and lay leadership positions
3. Does not allow for members of the Rabbinical or Cantorial Assemblies to perform commitment ceremonies for gays and lesbians
4. Does not allow for the Rabbinical or Cantorial schools to knowingly admit sexually active homosexual students, nor can they be admitted to either the Rabbinical Assembly or Cantors Assembly. (It did say that the schools would not begin investigations against students who are already students or members.)

5. Allowed for individual Rabbis within Conservative Movement institutions to determine whether or not sexually active homosexuals can function as teachers and youth leaders in the congregations.

What should synagogues do to become more welcoming to people in a homosexual relationship?

Rabbi Dorff explains:

"As Conservative synagogues take steps to make gays and lesbians feel welcome within our midst, gays and lesbians, like heterosexuals, have the duty to strive to live by the virtues [see pages 131-132] in all of their relationships, including sexual ones.....Furthermore, like all other Jews, gays and lesbians have the duties of Jewish study and action, including affiliation and active participation in a synagogue and in the Jewish community generally."
(Rabbinic Letter, page 42)

The Commission on Human Sexuality of the Conservative Movement made the following recommendations.

1. Meet with gay and lesbian Jews to sensitize synagogue members to that fact that there are those who should be welcomed into our communities who may not feel they are.

2. Special Interest or programs geared toward specific target audiences (example: first time parent programs), may include a gay or lesbian group in the synagogue program.

3. School educators may include homosexuality education in their curriculum on sexuality and Judaism where the issue is studied and discussed in order to raise awareness on the issues and people involved.

4. Synagogues may organize social action programs to advance the civil protection of gays and lesbians.

In this chapter we discussed the idea that our bodies are holy and how we present ourselves is important. We discussed the idea of infatuation versus love and the importance of being able to distinguish between the two. Sexual relations within a marriage rises to the level of holiness when both partners desire each other and consent to the relations. Teenagers may feel pressure to engage in sexual activity and we discussed those pressures and some ways to respond to them. We also sought to discuss attitudes in the Conservative movement toward homosexual activity.

Part Four:

Beauty and Its Beast
Conflict and Relationships

In a final discussion on the relationships *bein adam l'chavero*, we will learn about the high value Judaism places on creating peaceful and harmonious relationships. Recognizing that conflict is a part even of healthy relationships, we also will discuss some of the ways that communication can help to diminish conflict. Cliques and bullying are destructive to relationships and although they may seem like normal behavior they are unacceptable. Many of us are bystanders to these forms of relational aggression and have opportunities to intervene. Exerting power and control over a partner is taboo and Jewish texts that support this are provided. Partner abuse is an extreme form of bullying and the chapter explores the dynamics of partner abuse and how to help a friend who may be experiencing abuse.

Chapter Eleven
harmony and conflict

הלל ושמאי קיבלו מהם הלל אומר הוי
כתלמידיו של אהרן אוהב שלום ורודף שלום
אוהב את הבריות ומקרבן לתורה

Hillel taught: Be a disciple of Aaron: loving peace and pursuing peace, loving your fellow creatures and attracting them to the study of Torah.

(Pirkei Avot 1:12)

Why do we need both parts of the first text? What is the difference between "loving" peace and "pursue" peace?

While we are required to love peace and to be a peaceful person, the text requires us to actively pursue peace. We can do this by ensuring that our words and interactions are peaceful and do not create conflict and we should help others achieve the same. We are required to avoid conflict, and to resolve conflict when it occurs.

This is one of the few commandments that does not have a qualifier. That is to say, there aren't particular situations that might or might not call for pursuing peace; it is something we are supposed to do all of the time, something that should be a constant action in our lives.

The Aaron mentioned in the text is the brother of Moses, and although he does not get as much recognition as his famous brother in Torah stories, he plays the important role of a spiritual leader.

The Zohar, a book of mystical matters in Judaism, tells us that Aaron was chosen to be the *Kohain Gadol*, high priest, because of his commitment to peace and tranquility. If Aaron saw two people arguing, he would speak to each person separately and tell them, "Your friend feels really bad that you are having a disagreement, and wants to make up and be friends again." In this manner when the two friends saw each other again, they would patch up their dispute and be friends again.

How did Aaron's commitment to peace make him the best candidate for a spiritual leader?

Think back to the discussion about judging a person favorably.
How is that a good policy for ensuring peace?

What does it mean to "pursue peace?" How do we do that?

Shalom Bayit

Judaism places a great deal of value on the concept of "shalom bayit"—literally translated as "peace in the home."

Does "home" only refer to our physical houses? What else could it refer to? Should we only seek peace for ourselves? What about others who are in conflict?

Home can also mean our emotional spaces—our social circles, circles of friends, and our communities at large. We have a responsibility to help ensure that peace exists in all of these places.

How can we help encourage peace in our homes?

Reacting vs. Responding

Often a person will react to a conflict with his or her gut, rather than stopping to think about an appropriate response. This can cause the conflict to escalate and may hurt chances of resolving conflict.

Which is better for resolving conflict? Responding or reacting?
How does reacting with your gut impact the situation?
How does responding with your brain impact the situation?

For each of the scenarios below and on the next page, write down what you think would be a gut reaction and then a thoughtful response. Then, find a friend and role play these situations, first using the gut reaction and then the thoughtful response.

You walk into your room to find your sister using your laptop without permission.

Gut reaction: _____
Thoughtful response: _____

You get to the basketball court and find your friends have started playing without you.

Gut reaction: _____
Thoughtful response: _____
Your significant other tells you she has accepted an invitation to a party you already said you didn't want to go to.

Gut reaction: _____
Thoughtful response: _____

Were there different outcomes for the situation depending on the reaction v. response?
Which situation had the more positive outcome?

Conflict in Friendships and Relationships

In the previous chapters, we talked a lot about words and the importance of good and constructive communication, as well as some methods to ensure positive communication.

Healthy communication is especially important when it comes to conflict. Disagreements and arguments are going to happen in any relationship; what defines your relationship as healthy is the ability to talk it through, and figure out a solution that is beneficial to and accepted by both partners, as peace is the ultimate goal.

Activity: Role Play: Escalating Conflict

Often arguments escalate, meaning that the disagreement may start off as fairly minor but will get progressively worse over the course of the argument. Find a friend and role play the following scenarios. Pay attention to how the arguments escalate over the course of the scene.

Person 1 needs a reference book to finish an assignment due right after study hall. Person 2 is using the reference book right now, but is working on an assignment due next week.

Person 1:   I really need to use that book to finish up my homework assignment.
Person 2:   But I'm using it right now. I'm working on an assignment too.
Person 1:   But mine is due first; yours isn't due until next week.
Person 2:   So? You shouldn't have waited until the last minute
Person 1:   I have a life. What can I say? Give me the book.
Person 2:   (pauses) But I got it first.
Person 1:   Don't be such a jerk! You can use it after me. I need it now!
Person 2:   So do I.
Person 1:   No you don't. What is wrong with you?
Person 2:   Look, I can't help it. Library rules. First come, first served.
Person 1:   Wait until I tell everyone that you did this to me. Your life is going to be over.

- What happens in this scene?
- Who is "at fault" here?
- How does the situation escalate? Are there specific words or phrases that contribute to the escalation of the argument?
- Were the people here using gut reactions or thoughtful responses?
- How could Person 1 have prevented the situation from escalating? How could Person 2 have prevented the situation from escalating?

Now, let's take a look at a scenario between two people who are dating:

Beth and David have been dating for two years. They argue a lot, often about little things. Today, Beth is canceling plans with David so she can hang out with her friend Sarah, who has been having problems with her boyfriend, Michael.

Beth: I'm really sorry, but Sarah has been down lately and she wants to hang out.

David: She's always "feeling down." She's such a needy friend.

Beth: That isn't nice. You know she and Michael have been having problems.

David: Michael doesn't think they're having problems. Sarah makes a big deal of everything.

Beth: That's not fair. Michael doesn't treat her right.

David: What? He's so good to her. She's just difficult.

Beth: Don't talk about my friend like that! You always do that, I hate it.

David: Well maybe you should get better friends, and then I wouldn't need to.

Beth: You are such a jerk. I don't want to talk to you right now. I'm going to find Sarah.

David: Fine! My friends are more fun than you anyways.

- What happens in this scene?
- Who is "at fault" here?
- How does the situation escalate? Are there specific words or phrases that contribute to the escalation of the argument?
- Were Beth and David using gut reactions or thoughtful responses?
- How could Beth have prevented the situation from escalating? David?

Role play both scenarios again, but this time, rewrite them so the situations end with a mutually beneficial resolution.

Activity- A Second Look

Underline the words that may have sparked or perpetuated the escalating argument. Under the 'harmful column', list those words. Under the 'helpful' column, suggest other phrases that could have been used.

Harmful	Helpful

Relational Aggression: Cliques and Bullying

There are benefits to conforming and being part of a community, but sometimes, standards of conformity can lead to the development of cliques. In addition, it can be a struggle to maintain individuality and stay part of a community at the same time.

What words come to mind when you hear someone say "clique?"

Clique [klik] *noun*

A small, exclusive group of people

Activity: Cliques

Think about the cliques in your school. What are the different cliques you can think of? Do all the schools have the same cliques?

List some of the cliques in your school:

_____

_____

_____

How did these groups form? What does it feel like not to belong to one of them?

Are they based on stereotypes (e.g. "math nerds") or based on talents or skills ("jocks")? Why do people join cliques (an exclusive group of people that leaves others out) and what are the effects of a clique on the individual and on the community?

Activity: Outsiders

We've all experienced what it feels like to be on the "outside." Think of a time when you've felt left out. List the feelings associated with being on the outside of a certain circle.

How do you think it feels for someone to be left out of a group or clique? What is the difference between a clique and a group of friends with similar interests? What effects can cliques have on a social community?

Activity: Cliques and Community

On the inside circle, write words for how cliques affect the individual. Within the outside circle, write how cliques affect the community.

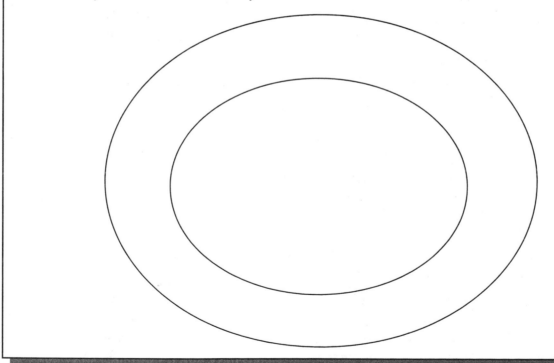

Mean in the Movies

As in the 2004 movie "Mean Girls," many adolescents have perfected the lunchroom snub and the art of vicious gossiping. In the movie, Janis, the first girl to befriend new student "Cady", reads the list of major cliques in high school: "You got your freshmen, ROTC guys, preps, J.V. jocks, Asian nerds, Cool Asians, Varsity jocks, Unfriendly black hotties, Girls who eat their feelings, Girls who don't eat anything, Desperate wannabes, Burnouts, Sexually active band geeks, the greatest people you will ever meet, and the worst. Beware of plastics." As she lists the seating plan by clique, the sound effects enhance the scene by incorporating jungle noises.

Is a jungle a good analogy for how cliques divide or destroy the social atmosphere of a school? The film is a comedy but is it also a true depiction of high school life? Is this the way your school is?

- *What do you think it feels like to be part of a clique?*
- *What do you think it feels like to be excluded from a clique?*
- *What does the structure of a clique look like? Are there leaders and followers?*
- *What determines if someone is a leader or a follower?*
- *Is there any function that a clique performs that helps the larger community?*
- *Are cliques tolerated? Why or why not?*

Think of some times when you have been part of or excluded from a clique and share some of these real life experiences with the group. Role play how the victim felt and how the insiders felt. Think about different ways that the experience could have been played out and the different possible outcomes.

Feeling Left Out

Have you ever felt left out of a social group?
Think about the social circles in your high school. One minute you could be "in," the next, you could be "out." Cliques are not the truest form of friendship and can cause feelings of inferiority and inadequacy.

Activity: Who Gets Picked?

You are putting together a baseball team of 13 players (male and female). Who would you choose to be on your team and who would you leave out? Why would you want certain players on your team and certain players left out? This activity will help you understand why people are chosen while others are left out. There are certain "desirable character traits" in a social setting which change constantly.

Physical Phil	Yelling Yael	Know-it-All Nelly
Cognitive Claire	Knowledgeable Ned	Friendly Fred
Passion Paul	Determined Dan	Angry Anna
Flexible Fanny	Assertive Adam	Athletic Amy
Jolly Jules	Passive Pam	Healthy Harry
Sad Sam	Energetic Erin	Excited Ellyn
Silent Sharon	Aggressive Aaron	Anxious Alyson

Remember: Cliques are exclusive clubs whose only real purpose is to make their members feel superior to nonmembers. While it is okay to have your own group of friends, it is never okay to be intolerant, exclusive, or disrespectful or judgmental. It is important to keep an open mind with your peers. You should never feel comfortable sitting and laughing with a large group of friends, while someone is sitting by him or herself. Put yourself in the shoes of someone who has been excluded, think about what that must feel like, and recognize that you could be that person tomorrow. Then get up, go over, and say hello.

Bullying

It may surprise teens to learn that cliques and bullying are closely related. Relational aggression is a type of bullying where social relations are used as the means to harm a peer, and while this may not be the sole reason that cliques are formed, it is certainly a common outcome of a clique.

Before we can talk about bullying, let's find out what it is:

Let's look at the narrative of Jacob and Esau:

כט וַיָּזֶד יַעֲקֹב, נָזִיד; וַיָּבֹא עֵשָׂו מִן-הַשָּׂדֶה, וְהוּא עָיֵף.	29 And Jacob sod pottage; and Esau came in from the field, and he was faint.
ל וַיֹּאמֶר עֵשָׂו אֶל-יַעֲקֹב, הַלְעִיטֵנִי נָא מִן-הָאָדֹם הָאָדֹם הַזֶּה—כִּי עָיֵף, אָנֹכִי; עַל-כֵּן קָרָא-שְׁמוֹ, אֱדוֹם.	30 And Esau said to Jacob: 'Let me swallow, I pray thee, some of this red, red pottage; for I am faint.' Therefore was his name called Edom.
לא וַיֹּאמֶר, יַעֲקֹב: מִכְרָה כַיּוֹם אֶת-בְּכֹרָתְךָ, לִי.	31 And Jacob said: 'Sell me first your birthright.'
לב וַיֹּאמֶר עֵשָׂו, הִנֵּה אָנֹכִי הוֹלֵךְ לָמוּת; וְלָמָּה-זֶּה לִי, בְּכֹרָה.	32 And Esau said: 'Behold, I am at the point to die; and what profit shall the birthright do to me?'
לג וַיֹּאמֶר יַעֲקֹב, הִשָּׁבְעָה לִּי כַּיּוֹם, וַיִּשָּׁבַע, לוֹ; וַיִּמְכֹּר אֶת-בְּכֹרָתוֹ, לְיַעֲקֹב.	33 And Jacob said: 'Swear to me first'; and he swore unto him; and he sold his birthright unto Jacob.
לד וְיַעֲקֹב נָתַן לְעֵשָׂו, לֶחֶם וּנְזִיד עֲדָשִׁים, וַיֹּאכַל וַיֵּשְׁתְּ, וַיָּקָם וַיֵּלַךְ; וַיִּבֶז עֵשָׂו, אֶת-הַבְּכֹרָה.	34 And Jacob gave Esau bread and pottage of lentils; and he did eat and drink, and rose up, and went his way. So Esau despised his birthright.

(Bereishit 25:29-34)

Did Jacob bully his brother Esau into giving him what he wanted, knowing how vulnerable Esau was?

Think about the narrative of Jacob's son Joseph and his brothers:

ג וְיִשְׂרָאֵל, אָהַב אֶת-יוֹסֵף מִכָּל-בָּנָיו—כִּי-בֶן-זְקֻנִים הוּא, לוֹ; וְעָשָׂה לוֹ, כְּתֹנֶת פַּסִּים.

3 Now Israel loved Joseph more than all his children, because he was the son of his old age; and he made him a coat of many colors.

ד וַיִּרְאוּ אֶחָיו, כִּי-אֹתוֹ אָהַב אֲבִיהֶם מִכָּל-אֶחָיו—וַיִּשְׂנְאוּ, אֹתוֹ; וְלֹא יָכְלוּ, דַּבְּרוֹ לְשָׁלֹם.

4 And when his brethren saw that their father loved him more than all his brethren, they hated him, and could not speak peaceably unto him.

(Bereishit 37:3-4)

Joseph's brothers are jealous of their father's love for Joseph. Eleven brothers against one, they conspire to kill him:

יח וַיִּרְאוּ אֹתוֹ, מֵרָחֹק; וּבְטֶרֶם יִקְרַב אֲלֵיהֶם, וַיִּתְנַכְּלוּ אֹתוֹ לַהֲמִיתוֹ. יט וַיֹּאמְרוּ, אִישׁ אֶל-אָחִיו: הִנֵּה, בַּעַל הַחֲלֹמוֹת הַלָּזֶה—בָּא.

18 And they saw him afar off, and before he came near unto them, they conspired against him to slay him. **19** And they said one to another: 'Behold, this dreamer cometh.

כ וְעַתָּה לְכוּ וְנַהַרְגֵהוּ, וְנַשְׁלִכֵהוּ בְּאַחַד הַבֹּרוֹת, וְאָמַרְנוּ, חַיָּה רָעָה אֲכָלָתְהוּ; וְנִרְאֶה, מַה-יִּהְיוּ חֲלֹמֹתָיו.

20 Come now therefore, and let us slay him, and cast him into one of the pits, and we will say: An evil beast hath devoured him; and we shall see what will become of his dreams.'

כא וַיִּשְׁמַע רְאוּבֵן, וַיַּצִּלֵהוּ מִיָּדָם; וַיֹּאמֶר, לֹא נַכֶּנּוּ נָפֶשׁ.

21 And Reuben heard it, and delivered him out of their hand; and said: 'Let us not take his life.'

כב וַיֹּאמֶר אֲלֵהֶם רְאוּבֵן, אַל-תִּשְׁפְּכוּ-דָם—הַשְׁלִיכוּ אֹתוֹ אֶל-הַבּוֹר הַזֶּה אֲשֶׁר בַּמִּדְבָּר, וְיָד אַל-תִּשְׁלְחוּ-בוֹ: לְמַעַן, הַצִּיל אֹתוֹ מִיָּדָם, לַהֲשִׁיבוֹ, אֶל-אָבִיו.

22 And Reuben said unto them: 'Shed no blood; cast him into this pit that is in the wilderness, but lay no hand upon him'—that he might deliver him out of their hand, to restore him to his father.

כג וַיְהִי, כַּאֲשֶׁר-בָּא יוֹסֵף אֶל-אֶחָיו; וַיַּפְשִׁיטוּ אֶת-יוֹסֵף אֶת-כֻּתָּנְתּוֹ, אֶת-כְּתֹנֶת הַפַּסִּים אֲשֶׁר עָלָיו. כד וַיִּקָּחֻהוּ—וַיַּשְׁלִכוּ אֹתוֹ, הַבֹּרָה; וְהַבּוֹר רֵק, אֵין בּוֹ מָיִם.

23 And it came to pass, when Joseph was come unto his brethren, that they stripped Joseph of his coat, the coat of many colors that was on him; **24** and they took him, and cast him into the pit—and the pit was empty, there was no water in it.

(Bereishit 37:18-24)

The brothers have a change of heart and decide to sell Joseph to a caravan of Ishmaelites traveling through:

כו וַיֹּאמֶר יְהוּדָה, אֶל-אֶחָיו: מַה-בֶּצַע, כִּי נַהֲרֹג אֶת-אָחִינוּ, וְכִסִּינוּ, אֶת-דָּמוֹ.

26 And Judah said unto his brethren: 'What profit is it if we slay our brother and conceal his blood?

כז לְכוּ וְנִמְכְּרֶנּוּ לַיִּשְׁמְעֵאלִים, וְיָדֵנוּ אַל-תְּהִי-בוֹ, כִּי-אָחִינוּ בְשָׂרֵנוּ, הוּא; וַיִּשְׁמְעוּ, אֶחָיו.

27 Come, and let us sell him to the Ishmaelites, and let not our hand be upon him; for he is our brother, our flesh.' And his brethren hearkened unto him.

(Bereishit 37:26-27)

(The portion of the narrative concludes with Reuben returning later to the pit to find that Joseph was gone. The brothers soak his coat in blood before bringing it to Jacob who assumes Joseph has died.)

Did Jacob's children learn to bully from him?

Was this bullying or sibling rivalry?

How do you think Joseph feels? What sparked this behavior from the brothers?
Why do you think that jealousy may often be the underlying root of bullying? What else might a bully want?

What is bullying and why do people pick on others?

Definition: A bully is someone who repeatedly intimidates, offends, degrades, insults or humiliates. Bullying can be physical, verbal (name-calling, taunting, insulting), or emotional (alliance building, silent treatment, shunning, spreading nasty gossip and online or cyber-bullying). It is deliberate and hurtful behavior, usually repeated over a period of time. Bullying is almost always done to kids who are perceived to be vulnerable.

We may think of a bully as a big kid on a playground beating up on smaller kids. That is a type of bullying but here we are talking about situations where social relationships are used as the means to harm a peer. This is also called 'relational aggression.' There are so many examples of this type of bullying in many of the reality television shows that it might seem that acting this way is 'normal' and desirable. For example, the show *Gossip Girl* is filled with the high drama of exclusionary behaviors, deliberately pitting people against each other creating tension and isolation and intimidation through gossip, unspoken rules, and threats. The glamorous characters of the show may make it seem like this behavior is 'cool' and ordinary teens may think it is acceptable to mimic their behaviors.

- *How do peer pressure and cliques contribute to bullying? If you're different from us, you're a target.*
- *Do you agree that television glamorizes 'relational aggression'?*
- *Is this type of bullying common at your school or with your friends? Discuss some experiences.*
- *What do you think it feels like to be the victim? The aggressor? The bystander?*
- *Why do you think teens bully each other?*
- *Do you think this is normal acceptable behavior?*

Activity: Barnyard Bullies

Returning to the jungle metaphor, choose any animal. Write out the strengths of that animal. Is the animal prey (pursued by other bigger, stronger animals) or a predator? What are its strengths and weaknesses?

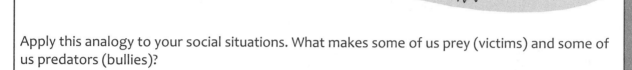

My animal is:

Strengths:

Apply this analogy to your social situations. What makes some of us prey (victims) and some of us predators (bullies)?

What animal have you been?

If you were once a bully — what makes you choose to bully?

If you were (or are currently) being bullied, what made you accept the bullying without asserting yourself? Why do victims of bullying not stand up for themselves?

We live in a jungle of different types of personalities/people (i.e. animals in a barn), how can you work to embrace each of the strengths from the different animals even if they may be mentally or physically weaker than you?

Let's think about the impacts of being a victim of bullying. Relational aggression harms everyone involved – the victim, the aggressor and the bystanders. Victims often suffer deeply and may think about suicide – and have problems with relationships long into adulthood. (We are now learning that similarly aggressors also may be suicidal and have problems with relationships long into adulthood).

What about the people who observe this aggression? How are they affected?

Three scenarios are given below. Read and or/role play them and discuss:

Scenario 1

Claire is the new girl in school. Ever since she started a few weeks ago, Rachel, the most popular girl in school, has been picking on her. In the lunch room, Claire walks by and Rachel says "Wow, she can't even choose a matching outfit! What a loser." Everyone around laughs. Claire turns red and finds an empty table in the corner to eat her lunch.

What is Rachel doing in this scenario?
Why should we care? What effect does this behavior have on the kids around them?
How do the bystanders ("everyone around laughs") in this story contribute to the problem?
What do you think would have happened if someone had told Rachel her name-calling and teasing wasn't nice and to stop doing it?
What could you do to help Claire?

Brainstorm: What can you do to help Rachel stop bullying?

Rachel is an example of a bully (בריון) someone who repeatedly teases and picks on other kids. She is trying to make Claire feel bad about herself by making fun of her. Bullies pick on people whom they think are weak – perhaps because they are different from the majority of kids and/or because the victim appears to lack confidence in her or himself.

Scenario 2:

Jake would not be considered one of the "cool" kids at his day school. He is having a hard time keeping up in his classes, his parents are separating, and money is tight so he wasn't able to go to camp last summer or on an Israel trip, or get his own car like everyone else in his well-off suburban neighborhood. Jake has never been good at sports and he is self-conscious about his acne and his height. In short, life is horrible and hard for Jake and just when it seemed that his sophomore year couldn't possibly get any worse, his friends turned on him. Suddenly, it seems that none of the three guys he has been buddies with since kindergarten want anything to do with him. They aren't able to hang out after school, avoid him on weekends, and the lunch table where they had always sat together now doesn't have room for him. Pictures were posted on his homepage of him in embarrassing situations with captions calling him a "loser." People commented on the photos agreeing with the caption and name-calling and teasing has resulted. To add to his computer issues, he had told one of his so-called friends his password to his email and now embarrassing emails that look like they're from him are being sent to the all the girls in the class asking them out and telling them how hot he thinks they are. Totally humiliated, Jake feels lost and alone.

What should he do?

Scenario 3

Jesse is scared. Ever since he was 12, he has had a sneaking suspicion that he might be gay and now, after spending a summer in camp, living in a small crowded bunk with 10 other guys, he thinks he really might be. Jesse is not ready to talk about this or share his feelings with anyone yet, but his 'friends' are eager to. Suddenly, Jesse is fair game and comments like "no gays at this table" greet him when he wants to sit down at lunch. When the teacher assigned partners for chemistry lab, everyone refused to be matched with Jesse with comments like "I don't want to be with a homo," "I don't want him to get a crush on me," "I don't want to catch anything gay." He keeps getting texts with words like 'fag' and 'queer' and his 'friends' on line are posting nasty messages about him and photo-shopping pictures of him with other guys. Jesse had really been looking forward to Winter Convention but now that it's clear that no one will want to room with him or talk to him he isn't sure if he should even go. Jesse had always loved school and his friends and USY and now he feels threatened, alone, humiliated and scared. What can Jesse do? What should the school do?

What should you do?

Tips for bullying victims:

What do you think are the most effective ways to counter bullies? Bullies gain their power when the victim reacts to the bullying – they hate being ignored. Brainstorm ways to deal with the situation.

Some tips are to:
- Believe in yourself.
- Ignore the bully, walk away from the situation, don't get physical, think about how it makes you feel, talk about it with your friends, guidance counselor, parents, doctors, or any trusted adult.
- Think about what you can do to gain confidence – ask yourself, what can I do to feel good about myself – maybe join a club and get involved in new activities, exercise, volunteer, play a sport, get an after school job, raise your grades, or make new friends.

Being a Bystander

Earlier in this chapter, we talked about responsibility—we are responsible for the consequences of the actions we choose. Are we responsible for the consequences of an action that someone else did, but we did not stop?

People who witness bullying behavior are called bystanders and often have an opportunity to speak up and challenge the bully. Bystanders often say that they are scared to say or do something – they are afraid to make the person angry and are afraid that if they do, they will make the situation worse. But actually, there are often many opportunities and many people who can intervene. All of us have a chance to help create safe communities, communities that do not allow any type of violence to take place.

"But it's not my problem…" or is it?

טז לֹא-תֵלֵךְ רָכִיל בְּעַמֶּיךָ, לֹא תַעֲמֹד עַל-דַּם רֵעֶךָ: אֲנִי, יְהוָה. **16** You shall not go up and down as a talebearer among thy people; neither shall you stand idly by the blood of your neighbor: I am the Lord.

(Vayikra 19:16)

A person who loves a friend cannot stand by and watch that friend be beaten or insulted.
The person would come to the friend's aid.
(Rabbi Moshe Chaim Luzzato, Mesilat Yesharim 19:17)

Recall previous text:

כל ישראל ערבים זה בזה   All of Israel is responsible for one another

(Talmud, Shevuot 39a)

- *Do you agree with these texts that it is a friend's responsibility to step in?*
- *In what ways can we demonstrate that we are all responsible for one another?*
- *How is helping a victim of bullying an example of **Derech Eretz**, the concept we discussed in a previous chapter on ethical living?*
- *Why would one be afraid to intervene as a bystander in a bullying situation?*

Let's take a look at some biblical bystanders who chose to act.

יא וַיְהִי בַּיָּמִים הָהֵם, וַיִּגְדַּל מֹשֶׁה וַיֵּצֵא אֶל-אֶחָיו, וַיַּרְא, בְּסִבְלֹתָם; וַיַּרְא אִישׁ מִצְרִי, מַכֶּה אִישׁ-עִבְרִי מֵאֶחָיו. **11** And it came to pass in those days, when Moshe was grown up, that he went out unto his brethren, and looked on their burdens; and he saw an Egyptian smiting a Hebrew, one of his brethren.

יב וַיִּפֶן כֹּה וָכֹה, וַיַּרְא כִּי אֵין אִישׁ; וַיַּךְ, אֶת-הַמִּצְרִי, וַיִּטְמְנֵהוּ, בַּחוֹל. **12** And he looked this way and that way, and when he saw that there was no man, he smote the Egyptian, and hid him in the sand.

(Shmot 2:11-12)

What message does Moshe send with his actions?

How about the story of David and Goliath? In Shmuel I, Chapter 17 we read that Goliath is taunting and threatening the men of Israel, the men of Israel are 'dismayed and terrified' and unable to act. David is a bystander, who chooses to act. What other choice could David have made? Was there pressure on him to make those other choices? His brother was mad at him, the troops didn't help him and the king told him that he was only a boy and could not fight a warrior.

As mentioned earlier, there are many reasons why someone may choose to bully others. Here we have a traditional Jewish text describing how one should treat the bully itself and not the behavior. It is controversial. Read it and agree or disagree:

הנהו בריוני דהוה בשיבבותיה דרבי זירא, דהוה מקרב להו כי היכי דניהדרו להו בתיובתא. והוו קפדי רבנן. כי נח נפשיה דרבי זירא אמרי: עד האידנא הוה חריכא קטין שקיה דהוה בעי עלן רחמי, השתא מאן בעי עלן רחמי? הרהרו בלבייהו, ועבדו תשובה.

In the neighborhood of R. Zera there lived some bullies. He nevertheless showed them friendship in order to lead them to repent; but the Rabbis were annoyed [at his action]. When R. Zera died they said: Until now we had the burnt man with the short legs to implore Divine mercy for us; who will do so now for us? Thereupon they felt remorse in their hearts and repented.

(Babylonian Talmud Sanhedrin 37a)

What's the story here? What is the moral?

- *Why would Rabbi Zera show friendship to a bully?*
- *Would you want to befriend someone who bullied others?*
- *How could kindness change a bully's behavior?*
- *Should you treat someone with kindness who treats others with disrespect?*

If you intervene with a bully, or even befriend a bully, your actions may be considered risky or bold, but in trying to respect the bully, you are showing him/her the importance of caring for others. Often, a bully seeks compassion and friendship but only knows how to interact through aggressive behavior. You do not need to become best friends with a bully but your kind actions may lead him/her to soften and learn to appreciate others. Or, it may do nothing at all and the bully may continue his/her behavior. When it comes to interacting with a bully, your actions come down to choice. You have the choice how to respond to any given situation. With confidence and mature, rational thinking, you will decide the right thing to do.

Thinking about why bystanders do or do not intervene
Bystanders who choose not to intervene become caught in the crossfire, de-sensitized, and become part of the bullying.

- *What do you think is the responsibility of a bystander?*
- *Do you think it is realistic to intervene?*
- *What factors would make this very challenging? Are there things you can do to make it less difficult to intervene?*
- *What are some ways for a bystander to intervene – think of some concrete strategies.*
- *Is a bystander responsible if he or she does speak up when seeing someone behaving inappropriately?*

Cyberbullying

Cyberbullying is a new way of bullying and it can be far more devastating than in-person bullying —it spreads quickly and reaches far more people than in-person bullying ever could. It also allows the bully to be anonymous, if he/she wants to be. Cyberbullying is the willful and repeated use of electronic devices such as cell phones and computers to harass, intimidate and threaten others. Methods include texting, sexting, emailing, chat rooms, blogs, websites, sending photos, and posting fake profiles. (Sexting is broadcasting nude or semi-nude photos by cell phone text messaging. In 2009, legislators in at least eight states introduced legislation to deter sexting).

(The National Campaign to Prevent Teen and Unplanned Pregnancy and CosmoGirl.com. 2008. Sex and Tech: Results from a Survey of Teens and Young Adults. Available at http://www.thenationalcampaign.org/sextech/PDF/SexTech_Summary.pdf.)

Cyberbullying: Pushed to the Edge

Recently, there have been a number of tragedies involving teens who had online relationships with a person who misrepresented her- or himself.

This is a true story of a 13 year old girl in Missouri who killed herself after receiving nasty messages from a boy she had met online. It turned out that the boy was really the mother of a former friend who lived four houses down the street. Megan Meier had been flirting via her MySpace® account with 'Josh Evans' for a few weeks and then started getting nasty messages from him. The last message suggested that "the world would be a better place" without her. Megan, believing she had been rejected by "Josh," hanged herself in her home.

Six weeks after Megan's death, her parents learned that "Josh Evans" never existed. He was an online character created in order to harass her by Lori Drew, age 47, who knew that Megan had been prescribed anti-depression medication and that she had a MySpace® page, along with Lori's daughter who was a classmate of Megan and an 18 year old employee of that family.

(A federal grand jury indicted Ms. Drew in May 2008 on charges that she had used a phony online identity to trick and taunt Megan. She pled not guilty to the charges and the case went to trial in November 2008. She was convicted of three misdemeanor counts of computer fraud for having misrepresented herself on MySpace® . The conviction was overturned in July 2009 on the grounds that the particular law being used was vague and flawed).

- *What can we learn from this tragedy?*
- *Why do you think people choose to misrepresent themselves online?*
- *What should teens do to protect themselves from online relationships?*

Scenario 4:

Julie was thrilled to find out that she would become co-captain of her school's basketball team. Even though she and Kate, the current captain, never really got along, Julie was sure they could work together given their mutual love of the sport. But to her dismay, Julie got 30 text messages that day saying "u bttr wtch out!" and "u r a ho." Later that night, when checking her on line page, Julie noticed that she had fourteen unread messages; it didn't take long for her to lose her excitement when she saw that all of the messages were from teammates and friends of Kate telling Julie she did not deserve to be co-captain, that she was too fat to even be playing on the court, and that she was just trying to ruin Kate's life. One even accused her of sleeping with the coach to get her new position. The last message was from Kate herself, containing only a link. As Julie apprehensively clicked to the new webpage, Julie saw a fake account using her name and pictures of her head photo-shopped onto strippers' bodies. Julie was able to hold it all to-gether—until she realized that several teachers and college admission counselors kept in touch with her via her social networking site.

What should Julie do? You are Julie's friend – what can you do to help her?
Should there be any consequences for Kate, the teammates and friends? If yes, what? If no, why not?

Digital media has created a whole different playing field for bullies.
- **What makes internet bullying worse than face-to-face bullying?**
- **Can you ever recover bullying types that have been posted online?**
- **Can you share any personal stories about online bullying?**
- **What do you think parents, teens and teachers can do to help prevent online bullying? How can it be treated once it's out there?**

Lashon Hara and Digital Media case study:

Gossip (Lashon Hara) has become a major problem in your school and is flooding the internet. IM conversations are being passed around the entire student body after hours and no adult knows about it. Email rumors are being spread and social network sites are flooded with horrible comments about certain people in your school. This type of harassment is damaging, however more dangerous than before as no adult is aware of it.

What could become of a situation like this?

What should you do if you are being cyberbullied?

Brainstorm: What do you think are some ways to stop cyberbullying?

How do these scenarios connect back to our discussion on Lashon Hara and Shmirat Halashon?

Look back at the discussion on Shmirat Halashon and think about the a concept suggested on page 95 of "Shmirat Ha'etzba'ot" or guarding of the fingers.

How does this connect with what we can do about cyber bullying? What can we do?

- Do not respond - do not answer emails or respond to posts or chats
- Save the evidence – remember even when the bully is anonymous, there is always evidence left behind.
- Tell a friend.
- Tell an adult. A parent or other trusted adult should be told if you are being bullied. Cyber-bullying is no different than in-person bullying. If you think that the bully goes to your school, then tell a school official. Schools take bullying very seriously and many states now have laws prohibiting cyberbullying.
- If you get even one communication that includes a threat of bodily harm or a death threat the police should be alerted. Urging suicide is considered a death threat and the police will treat it accordingly.

Tips: Remember that there is no privacy online. Here's a rule that may be hard to keep—Don't type it unless you are prepared for it to be spread around. Don't share your passwords with anyone, even friends. Create strong passwords to reduce the chance of being hacked.

Chapter Twelve
When Love Hurts

Dating Abuse

Dating abuse shares many similarities with bullying, except that often the stakes are higher, the victim is more isolated, and the consequences more severe. Being betrayed by a dating partner who says he or she loves you, is often seen as the ultimate betrayal.

Until recently, this issue of dating abuse (as well as domestic abuse – abuse between partners) in the Jewish community was not discussed publicly. However because this is an issue that impacts so many American teens – in fact the age group in greatest danger of being victims of abuse are young people ages 16 – 24 – the Jewish community has begun to openly discuss this problem. However, we know that all too often, a teenager will not recognize the signs of abuse and will not know where to go for help.

Although we hope none of us will ever experience abuse in our dating relationships, it is an important issue to discuss and learn about. As you head off to college, you should also know that there are resources on your campus that can help anyone in an abusive relationship. You will be away from your family and friends but there will be trained and trustworthy adults on campus to turn to for help – either for yourself, or for a friend.

Shalom in the Home: Not Just a Reality TV Show

Judaism places a great deal of value on harmonious relationships between married partners – the concept known as 'shalom bayit' as mentioned in the last chapter. In Sefer Mishlei, The Book of Proverbs we read:

מְשׁוֹר   טוֹב אֲרֻחַת יָרָק, וְאַהֲבָה-שָׁם-- יז   17 Better is a dinner of herbs where love is,
אָבוּס, וְשִׂנְאָה-בוֹ.   than a fatted ox and hatred with it.
(Mishlei 15:17)

מִבַּיִת, מָלֵא   טוֹב פַּת חֲרֵבָה, וְשַׁלְוָה-בָהּ-- א   1 Better is a dry morsel, and quietness with it,
זִבְחֵי-רִיב.   than a house full of feasting with quarrels.
(Mishlei 17:1).

Look at these texts:

A husband should love his wife as much as he loves himself and should respect her more than he respects himself. (Yevamot 62B).

אמר רבי יוסי: מימי לא קריתי לאשתי
אשתי ולשורי שורי, אלא: לאשתי ביתי

Rabbi Yossi taught: I have never called my wife "my wife" rather, "my home."

(Talmud Shabbat 118b)

Respect between committed partners is a key concept in any Jewish home. The reality is however, that not all Jewish homes and filled with "shalom." Traditional Jewish texts did not condone any kind of abuse. Physical abuse was not permitted and there were severe repercussions for men who abused their wives and while there are some texts that do allow a husband to beat his wife to a certain degree, many texts prohibit such behavior.

"It is an accepted view that we have to treat a man who beats his wife more severely than we treat a man who beats another man, since he is not obligated to honor the other man but is obligated to honor his wife – more, in fact, than himself. And a man who beats his wife should be put under a ban and excommunicated and flogged and punished….
(Rabbi Yosef Caro, Even Ha-Ezer 154:15 quoting Rabbenu Simhah)

R. Perez b. Elijah wrote: "one who beats his wife is in the same category as one who beats a stranger"; he decreed that "any Jew may be compelled on application of his wife or one of her near relatives to undertake by a herem (threat of excommunication) not to beat his wife in anger or cruelty so as to disgrace her, for that is against Jewish practice."

Marital rape was prohibited (note that by contrast until recently marital rape was permitted in many states). And in the Talmud we learn: Rami b. Hama said in the name of Rav Assi: A man is forbidden to force his wife to have sex. Rambam said: He is not to have intercourse while drunk, nor in the midst of a quarrel, he is not to do so out of hate, nor may he take her by force with her in fear of him. (Maimonides, Laws of Marital Status, Hilchot Eishut 15:17)

Verbal and emotional abuse was also prohibited. In writing about marriage and marital relations, Maimonides wrote: "He is not to cast upon her extreme fear, he is not to intimidate her, he is not to say things which make her upset emotionally, which might cause her anxiety and discomfort. He must speak to her gently, he is not to be intense, sad, or angry." (Laws of Marital Status, Hilchot Eishut 15)

While these texts are all about married relationships, none of these behaviors is permitted in dating relationships either.

> **Definition:** Dating abuse is a pattern of coercive behaviors used to establish control over a dating partner. Abuse is not a one-time, accidental occurrence; abusers deliberately act in ways that establish power and control over a partner. However, unhealthy relationship characteristics may be warning signs or red flags that a relationship is headed towards dating abuse.

We've talked a lot about healthy relationship characteristics: Mutual respect, good communication, feelings of equality in actions and emotional expression, and the ability to work through disagreements and arguments. By contrast, in an unhealthy relationship there is a lack of respect and trust. A partner may feel afraid to express herself and unable to communicate in a healthy way to resolve conflict.

In a healthy relationship, both partners feel that they can share what they are feeling and thinking, they can communicate effectively to work through problems and find a mutually beneficial solution. In an unhealthy relationship, one partner may call the other names, put him or her down, cause embarrassment in public, or reveal something the partner did not want anyone else to know. These red flags are frequently warning signs of problems, and may be signs that the relationship either is or will become an abusive one.

Abusive behaviors in a relationship can be physical, verbal/emotional or sexual, as well as technological and abuse often manifests itself as a combination of all these behaviors.

Activity: Healthy or Unhealthy?

Put a check mark next to each unhealthy behavior on this list. Put a star next to anything you are not sure about.

___ Her boyfriend always wants to know where she is and who she is with
___ His partner sends him a text saying "I love you."
___ Her boyfriend buys her a gift after they have a big fight
___ His girlfriend calls him "stupid" in front of his friends
___ Her partner listens to her point of view during an argument
___ His girlfriend doesn't like it when he hangs out without her
___ Her boyfriend tells her "If you loved me, you'd have sex with me"
___ His partner posts an embarrassing picture of him on line.
___ Her boyfriend says "ok" when she tells him she does not want to have sex
___ His girlfriend tells her friends his secret she had promised not to tell anyone
___ His boyfriend tells him he will 'out' him if he doesn't quit talking to other guys
___ Her boyfriend gets angry if she doesn't text him back right away
___ Her partner says "ok" when she tells her she wants to hang out with her friends alone

Which behaviors did you mark as unhealthy? Which behaviors did you mark as healthy?
Were there any behaviors you were unsure about, or could be healthy or unhealthy depending on the context of the situation?

It may be difficult to tell which are red flags of abusive behavior and what would be considered "normal" behaviors of conflict. It is important that as you enter into dating situations, you learn to distinguish between normal conflict that can be resolved in a healthy way and abuse. In order to distinguish between the two, it helps to understand what abusive behavior looks like.

What Does Dating Abuse Look Like?

Physical Abuse

Physical abuse includes anything that involves physical violence, even if it does not result in any injury or leave any marks. Some examples of physical abuse are: Hitting, punching, pushing, kicking, slapping and biting. In the most extreme case, physical abuse can lead to death. One in five teens who have been in a serious relationship report being hit, slapped or pushed by a partner.

- He punched me in the face. I had to wear sunglasses the next day so nobody would see my black eye.
- She pushed me down the stairs; my arm was broken in three places.
- He grabbed me by my hair and yanked me up, yelling in my face.
- She grabbed a knife from the counter and stabbed me in the shoulder.

Emotional and Verbal Abuse

Emotional and verbal abuse make a partner feel like he or she is worthless, that nobody else would ever want him or her, that he or she is lucky to have the abuser as a partner, and that no one would believe him or her if they told anyone about the abuse. One-quarter of teens say they have been called names or put down by a dating partner. More than one in three teens reported that their partners wanted to know where they were and who they were with all the time. One in four teens who have been in a serious relationship say their partner has tried to prevent them from spending time with friends or family and to only spend time with their partner.

Emotional and verbal abusive behaviors include: name-calling and put-downs, intimidation, threats, coercion and manipulation, possessiveness, jealousy, control and violation of personal boundaries, and isolating from friends and support network.
- He said he'd tell everyone I was gay, if I wouldn't do sexual acts I wasn't ready to do.
- He wouldn't let me hang out with my friends unless he was there too.
- Whenever there were other guys around, he would make me hold his hand so everyone would know I belonged to him.
- I had to call or text him every hour on the hour; if I didn't, he'd come looking for me.
- She would get angry if she saw me talking to another girl.
- He would walk me to class and pick me up from class; I couldn't talk to a teacher even if I wanted to, he was always there.

Sexual Abuse

Sexual abuse can be as subtle as making lewd comments to a partner in public in a way that makes him or her uncomfortable, to not letting the partner use birth control or protection against sexually transmitted diseases and as serious as rape. One in eight teens say they have been pressured by a dating partner to engage in sexual activity when they did not want to.
- **Unwanted sexual touching**
    He would sometimes lift up my skirt in public.
    She would grab my crotch when we were at the mall or on the street.
- **Forced or coerced sexual activity**
    He would hold my head down and make me give him oral sex.
    She wouldn't let me use a condom, even though I wanted to.

Rape

- He would hold me down and force me to have sex.
- She once drugged me and tied me to the bed and forced me to have sex.

Use of Technology in Abusive Relationships

- Technology is used as a means of abusing victims emotionally and sexually.
- She would text me every half hour asking where I was and what I was doing.
- My cell phone became my electronic leash.
- He installed GPS into my cell phone and my car.
- He really wanted me to pose nude so that he could take a photo and have it forever. He wound up sending it around on email and posting in on Facebook®.

Statistics:

Teens report dating abuse via technology is a serious problem

71% of teens regard boyfriends/ girlfriends spreading rumors about them on cell-phones and social networking sites as a serious problem.

68% of teens say boyfriends/ girlfiends sharing private or embarrassing pictures/ videos on cell phones and computers is a serious problem.

Tech Abuse in Teen Relationships Study, Liz Claiborne (2007)

The Dynamics of Abuse

The dynamics of abuse are complicated. Few relationships start off with someone raping a dating partner, or even verbally abusing a dating partner. Abuse usually starts off slowly, subtly, and can escalate to epic and dangerous proportions, even resulting in maiming and death. Most frequently, abuse will start as verbal and emotional, and will escalate into physical and sexual.

While abuse is a pattern of behavior used to establish control over a dating partner, this does not mean that the pattern is consistent or regular.

Typically, in the beginning of the relationship, the abuse is non-existent, or so subtle the victim does not even notice. Then there is a conflict —maybe they get into a fight and he called her a bitch and a slut, telling her she's lucky to be dating him. Often, the couple will then make up but the abuse will most likely return and escalate, and then they will make up again. Each time, the verbal, physical and sexual abuse escalates and the honeymoon or make-up phase gets shorter until it almost disappears. At some point, the relationship no longer returns to its original honeymoon phase, which means that abuse is exists in some form all the time.

"But how could you hurt someone you love? I could never abuse someone."

Sound familiar? Think about the last time you got really angry at someone. Did you call them a name? Did you throw something? Did you hit your sibling recently? Anger is natural. It's learning to control our anger and channel it in different ways that can prevent even the most unlikely person from becoming a perpetrator of abuse.

Controlling Our Anger

But sometimes, she makes me so mad...I didn't mean to call her those names...I can't stand her whining....

Jewish value: Erech Apayim/ Slow to Anger (one of the Rambam's *13 Attributes of God*):

וְלֹא הַקַּפְּדָן מְלַמֵּד The angry person does not teach.

(Pirkei Avot 2:5)

Define this quote in terms of relationships. What words can be used instead of "teach?"

You can't get your point across when you're screaming, yelling or name--calling. When in conflict, you must learn to respond to the other person's conflicting belief and not react. A reaction may turn abusive; a response allows one to think rationally and responsibly.

We cannot control much of what is experienced but we can control how we respond to incidences. Violence and abuse is never the appropriate response, it is a reaction rooted in uncontrolled anger and frustration.

Activity: Responding vs. Reacting

How do you react to a trigger? Are you an emotional responder? Do you react physically (e.g. want to throw or break something)? Do you need to talk it out? Be alone? Deal with it on the spot?

Fill in the blanks:
When I get angry, the first thing I do is_____

The first thing I say is _____

It helps me to _____

Unfortunately, one thing I always do that doesn't really help is _____

_____

Identifying what triggers your reactions can help you control them. *How can we give our natural feelings of anger, jealousy or frustration toward another a safe and constructive purpose?*

Think about how you react to situations. Check off which would work for you:

- ☐ If you react to something physically—become a runner
- ☐ If you react to something emotionally—write out your feelings on paper or compose an email you'll never send (you tend to say things you may regret while ranting over email).
- ☐ If you react to something with harsh or loud words—count to ten or walk away and come back to the situation.

"Abuse happens to other people, not to me. I'm a tough guy/a strong woman…no one would ever treat me that way and get away with it."

Sometimes, even the toughest people can't let go.

Question: Why Doesn't The Victim Leave?

Many people, even friends and family of the victim, don't understand why a person in an abusive relationship doesn't just leave. Nobody goes out looking for an abusive relationship. Unhealthy and abusive behaviors escalate over time; an abuser will frequently wait until the partner is dependent, is isolated from his/ her support system, and has been belittled and put down to a point where he/ she truly believes he/ she is unworthy and lucky to have the abuser as a partner.

Leaving an abusive relationship is so much more than just walking out the door. There are a significant number of barriers that a person must first overcome before he/she can leave.

Brainstorm: What challenges might a person meet when trying to leave an abusive relationship?

Some responses might include fear and intimidation, shame, isolation, fear of being single, or love. Frequently, people who do not understand the dynamics of abuse will try to excuse the abusive behaviors, or not recognize them for what they are. Some ways that bystanders may try to "rationalize" what is happening is that the two people say they love each other or that the abuser has said "sorry."

As Jews, we can do *teshuva*, or repentance (literally "returning") when we do something wrong. But *teshuva* is more than just saying "I'm sorry." To truly do *teshuva*, we must admit we have done something wrong, do everything we can to rectify the hurt they have caused, and work on our behavior to ensure that it never happens again. Just saying the words "I'm sorry" isn't good enough.

Role Play: Helping a Friend

Statistics show that most victims of abuse will talk to a friend rather than anyone else. This means that a friend could come to you for help—would you know what to do or say? The most important things you can do are listen without blame; encourage the victim to seek help from a trusted adult – and – if the victim won't do that, then you, as a friend, must seek out that help for the victim. Even if your friend swore you to secrecy, if there is any chance that her life is in danger or she is being physically or sexually abused —you must tell an adult.

Never confront the abuser—this might put you and your friend in danger.

Activity: Assessing opportunities to intervene

Stopping an abuser and helping a victim is a community responsibility. There are many opportunities to intervene for a variety of bystanders. Read these scenarios (and/or act them out). Figure out who the bystanders are and how they could intervene. Remember to take into account what you know about the pattern of abuse, and the barriers to leaving an abusive relationship, and how bystanders can be helpful by intervening.

Scenario 1:

Jeremy and David have been dating for about a year and Jeremy told Carrie things are going really well—he thinks he's "the one!" Carrie is happy for Jeremy, but is a little worried about David. Jeremy is one of her best friends, but Carrie has noticed that Jeremy isn't always that nice to David. Sometimes he calls him names or makes fun of him in front of others, and when Jeremy is just with his friends he talks about him in a very derogatory manner. Last week, Carrie walked in on Jeremy and David having a fight—Jeremy was holding David very tightly by the arms and shaking him as he said: "You're lucky to be with me. Who else would want you?" David looked really scared, so Carrie asked him about it later. He told her it's not the first time they have had a fight like that, but he doesn't know what to do.

Scenario 2:

Sarah, a freshman at a medium-sized university, became very involved in school activities from the beginning. She quickly joined the dance company, held the freshman board position in school, and regularly volunteered at a local children's center, in addition to taking a full course load and balancing a job at an off-campus café. One Sunday at the children's center, she saw Phil, a cute junior in one of her classes, was also volunteering. After talking to him for a while, Sarah was taken with his sense of humor, apparent love for children, and his gorgeous smile. The next weekend, when she ran into him at a mutual friend's party, she was slightly concerned by how rough and visibly drunk he was acting with his guy buddies, but was ecstatic when he came over to talk to her and turned into a complete gentleman. Phil left the party with Sarah, and as he walked her to her dorm, asked her out on a date.

They went on several dates, and two weeks later Sarah called her mother excitedly to tell her that she was now "official" with Phil, a popular, pre-law, track star who was always "super sweet" and loved showing off that he was with Sarah, being sure to grab her hand in front of other guys; Sarah couldn't believe that she had found "the perfect guy." Her mother was surprised to hear all this from Sarah, who had always been focused on her studies and never fit the stereotypical girlfriend role.

Sarah and Phil became known as the perfect couple; he would cook for her in his campus apartment, they studied together, and he would even go shopping with her. On one trip to the local mall, they went into a store where Sarah's friend worked, she tried on a skirt, and he told her "you should try buying clothes that aren't slutty for once." He picked up a pair of awful baggy pants for her to try, but when she told him that she would just buy a pair of jeans she had pulled, he accused her of trying to lure other guys with her tight clothing. He was making such a scene in the store, not to mention in complete view of the cash register where Sarah's friend was working, that she gave in and ended up buying only the oversized pants. (continued on next page)

Slowly, Sarah wore more baggy clothing and less make-up, often only taking her hair out of a pony-tail for date nights with Phil. She also stopped meeting her friends for meals in the dining hall, opting instead to go over to Phil's, where he would often serve her smaller portions, saying that a girl who was with him needs to look in top condition. Sarah's dance professor suspected something when Sarah would get uncharacteristically tired before the end of every rehearsal. Sarah's grades dropped as she spent more time during lecture periods texting Phil instead of taking notes. Her friends noticed when her absences started occurring several times a week, and they stopped seeing her at parties and school events. When they called to check in or make plans, she either didn't answer, or could never talk for very long saying that "it's not the best time" and hang up. Her friends could often hear Phil yelling in the background as she ended her calls.

Sarah started to look forward to working at the café, because she felt it was her one legitimate excuse to be away from Phil without having to constantly call or text him to check in. But one evening, when a coworker called in sick and Sarah offered to stay later than usual to help her manager close up, Phil came storming in, asking why he hadn't heard from her yet, why she was ignoring him. She tried to calmly explain what happened—she didn't want her manager to think anything of their argument—but he threatened their relationship: "I don't need this, if you can't even be considerate of me while having a job then you better quit something, and you know no one else would want to date a whore like you." Sarah was deeply embarrassed and quickly finished her job while fighting back tears.

Being a friend to someone in an abusive or unhealthy relationship is important—talking to someone may be the first step to leaving the relationship. Leaving won't happen overnight—remember, there are many barriers to leaving an unhealthy or abusive relationship, but you, as a friend, can be the support your friend needs.

> If you find that you are in an abusive relationship, it is critical that you turn to a trusted adult —a USY advisor, a parent, a teacher, rabbi, doctor, guidance counselor, or camp counselor for help. Hotlines for free and confidential help are available also—just do an internet search and you'll find their toll free numbers. The most important thing to remember if you are in an abusive relationship is that you must get safe, you must tell someone you trust, and you can get out. The most important thing to remember if you think you are an abuser, or in danger of becoming one, is that you can get help too. Talk to a trusted adult and ask for help. It's important— your lives are at stake.

This chapter explored many aspects of conflict within relationships. While conflict in healthy relationships can often be resolved by good communication, it is always important to remember that compromising core values to maintain a relationship is unacceptable. Relational aggression is common among teens and may be seen as normal behavior. Cliques are groups that are based on excluding other people and are a form of bullying. Other forms of bullying behaviors are also explored, including cyber-bullying. Dating abuse is a further form of bullying behavior and is an extreme form of power and control over a partner. While there are many reasons why it is difficult to leave an abusive relationship, friends can be critical supports to the victim and may make it easier for the victim to leave. There are many opportunities for friends and other bystanders to intervene to stop all types of bullying. This is the responsibility of the entire community.

Chapter Thirteen
Decision making and peer pressure

In this chapter we will explore continue to explore the "bein adam l'atzmo" relationship and the "bein adam l'chavero" relationship. We will examine the steps to decision making, challenges to making a good decision, including peer pressure, and the importance of being strong and confident in our own beliefs and values. We have the ability to choose our actions but we must be mindful of the short- and long-term consequences at the same time.

יט הַעִדֹתִי בָכֶם הַיּוֹם, אֶת-הַשָּׁמַיִם וְאֶת-הָאָרֶץ--הַחַיִּים וְהַמָּוֶת נָתַתִּי לְפָנֶיךָ, הַבְּרָכָה וְהַקְּלָלָה; וּבָחַרְתָּ, בַּחַיִּים--לְמַעַן תִּחְיֶה, אַתָּה וְזַרְעֶךָ.

19 I call heaven and earth to witness against you this day: I have put before you life and death, blessing and curse. Choose life!

(D'varim 30:19)

What does this text tell us about free will and our ability to choose?

Throughout this book, you will notice a common theme that keeps emerging- that of your ability to choose. What distinguishes us, as humans, from animals is *bechira*—the ability to choose. We have the ability to see the difference between right and wrong, and the free will to make a decision about what we want to do.

The Freedom to Choose
Yetzer Hatov and Yetzer Hara

According to Jewish belief, human beings are created with two *yetzarim* or inclinations: Yezter Ha-tov and Yetzer Hara. Jewish tradition teaches a concept of an evil impulse, which it calls yetzer hara. This term is used to describe those temptations and challenges that humans are faced with and about which they have a choice. However, the Rabbis also recognize the existence of yetzer tov, or a good inclination. The Rabbis had much to say about the nature of the yetzer hara, the necessity to make choices, and choosing the right way. To understand these statements, we must be aware that while yetzer hara is often pictured as having an existence of its own, or in some cases is personified, such an explanation of the evil inclination is primarily a literary device.

 Yetzer Hatov- the good inclination- television usually depicts this "side" of a person as an angel.

Yetzer Hara- the inclination to make the wrong choice— usually depicted on TV as a devil.

Text 1:

דרש רב נחמן בר רב חסדא: מאי דכתיב (בראשית ב') וייצר ה' אלהים את האדם בשני יוד"ין - שני יצרים ברא הקדוש ברוך הוא, אחד יצר טוב ואחר יצר רע.

Rabbi Nachman Bar Rav Hisda explained: When it is written "and God creative created (yetzer) humanity, with two yuds," it is because God created two inclinations, one good inclination and one evil inclination.

(Talmud, Brachot 61a)

Text 2:

כך הקב"ה אמר להם לישראל: בני, בראתי יצר הרע ובראתי לו תורה תבלין, ואם אתם עוסקים בתורה - אין אתם נמסרים בידו

The Holy One of Blessed Being said to Israel: "my children, I created yetzer hara and I created for it the Torah as a solvent. And if you occupy yourselves with the story of Torah, then you will not be delivered to the evil inclination.

(Talmud, Kedushin 30b)

We have the power to choose which yetzer, which inclination, will win out in our decision making. This is considered free will.

What goes into making a choice?
What challenges are there when making a choice? How can we overcome the inclination to make a bad choice?

Life and death are pretty black and white choices—one is inherently good, while the other is inherently bad. **What happens when the choices are not so clear cut?**

The Decision Making Process

Think of a problem or situation recently where you had to make a decision or choice. How did you make that decision? Who influenced or inspired your decision? Were there steps you went through to come to your decision?

Activity: The Who of Decision Making

The Who: Consider who most influences your decisions. When I am faced with options, the fist "voice" I hear in my head is: *rank in order or check off the boxes*

☐ Me
☐ mom/dad
☐ my best friend
☐ an older sibling or cousin
☐ an aunt or uncle

☐ a teacher
☐ another trusted adult, a mentor
☐ a group of people (e.g. the popular clique at my school)
☐ media (movies, television, music)

Activity: The Who of Decision Making

Beside each example, write down **who** influences you in making your decision:

_____ Choosing what clothes to buy

_____ Deciding what music to listen to

_____ Responding to a rude remark

_____ Deciding what to eat

_____ Deciding how to spend free time

_____ Deciding how to speak /what to say to a member of the opposite sex

Peer Pressure

One of the aspects of belonging to any community is peer pressure—either by cultural value systems, family or friends, a community encourages you to behave in ways that sync up with and benefit the community, and discourages you from behaving in ways that do not positively impact the community.

Take the biblical prohibition for murder, stealing or engaging in shady business practices. All of those things are anti-social, meaning they negatively impact the greater community. Those behaviors are discouraged in order to preserve the community. Think back to our discussion about distancing oneself from an evil person—we can be influenced by someone even if we don't want to be, so it's better to just stay away.

Peer pressure can lead to odd, destructive, out-of-character behavior that you can't even explain. You're following someone else's actions without thinking about it.

Activity: Follow the Leader

This is a popular group game where everyone is seated in a circle. One person leaves the room and a leader is chosen. He/she makes continuous actions such as clapping or snapping and all others follow his/her lead. When he/she switches actions, all must follow. The person outside of the room must come back in and guess the leader.

Notice how your actions as a "mimic" of the leader are mechanical. You follow his/her actions without thinking or without making your own choice as to what to do next. Have you ever done something everyone else was doing without really thinking about it?

How can other people's actions and opinions impact the choices we make?

Do we often follow others without ever considering why we're doing what we do?

Consider new fashion trends: just because "everyone else is doing it/wearing it/saying it," does it mean that you should?

Do those opinions make it easier or harder to make a decision?

Think about a group you either belong to or hang out with regularly.
- *Are there rules about what people in that group are and are not allowed to do?*
- *Are there rules about who people in that group are and are not allowed to hang out with?*
- *Are there things people have to do to get into the group, or to stay in the group?*

Let's use our "Mean Girls" example again. Gretchen reminds Regina of the "rules" of the group:

> Gretchen: Regina, you're wearing sweatpants. It's Monday.
> Regina: So...?
> Karen: So that's against the rules, and you can't sit with us.
> Regina: Whatever. Those rules aren't real.
> Karen: They were real that day I wore a vest!
> Regina: Because that vest was disgusting!
> Gretchen: You can't sit with us!

Scenario 1

David is new in school. In his first few days, he sees all the different groups, and decides he wants to join the group that seems to be the most popular people in the school, but they pretty much ignore his attempts to be friends. One day, a bunch of guys in the group decide to cut class, and they ask David to join them.

Why do you think David wants to be part of that group?
What are the boys in the group doing to David?
Do you think that someone should have to "earn" admission to a group?
What do you think David should do?

Scenario 2

Becky is part of an elite circle of friends at her school. Her friends decide they are going to a party at one of the senior boys' houses upstate. Becky knows there will be alcohol and pot and doesn't want to go, but she knows that if she says no, her friends will make fun of her, and people will notice if she isn't there. She was going to spend the night at her friend's house anyway, so her parents would never know.

Becky is already part of this group, but she feels the need to maintain her "membership" by doing something she is not comfortable with. Why?
What is Becky worried will happen if she does not go to the party? Is that a legitimate worry?
What do you think Becky should do?

Both David and Becky want to be part of a special group, but they are challenged to make good decisions, even though that might jeopardize their position in the group (Becky), or their ability to enter into the group (David).

Sometimes we are faced with making a tough decision—standing up for our beliefs and standing out from everyone else, or following everyone else.
How can standing up for one's beliefs be challenging?
How can it be rewarding?

Activity: The How of Decision Making

How do you decide on things in your life?

Beside each example, write the **determining factor** to making your decision

_____ Choosing what clothes to buy

_____ Deciding what music to listen to

_____ Responding to a rude remark

_____ Deciding what to eat

_____ Deciding how to spend free time

_____ Deciding how to speak /what to say to a member of the opposite sex

Activity: Head, Heart or Mind

Think about it: Each time I make a decision, what parts of me are making that choice—head, heart, or mind?

Think about the last major decision you made.
Head—I've thought about it a little
Heart—I've considered my feelings
Mind—I've rationalized and considered consequences, weighed my options

For example: Choosing to do something with a friend:
My mind says I think it will be fun but my head says I'll be out late on a school night.

Attending a convention:
My heart is excited to see my friends. My head says I should stay home and fill out my college applications.

In the space below, write down a big decision you've recently made. Check off which part of you that you utilized to make that choice.

Recognizing the roots of your decisions will help you determine how you make your choices and where they come from. There are many factors that influence your decisions. It is important though, to make sure your decisions are informed and rooted in your values and feelings and not someone else's. These are obstacles in recognizing your ability and right to make your own life choices.

Although it is *your* life and ultimately, your choice, the people who surround you impact your decisions. You have the power to choose to be influenced by the positive forces in your life or to let negative influences overpower your free will. Even though others influence your decisions, you pay the price for any choices you make that may cause regret. Many people surround you, many voices may appear in your subconscious, but ultimately, the choice is yours. Then how do you come to any kind of decision when faced with options?

My steps to making a decision are:

1.	2.	3.
4.	5.	6.

"DEWS" The Decision Making Process

You may not realize, but a lot goes into making a decision, even if you do some of it unconsciously or very quickly. Let's break down the DEWS steps:

D: Define the dilemma: What is it you need to make a decision about?
E: Explore the options: What are all of the choices in this situation?
W: Weigh the consequences: Evaluate the consequences (positive and negative) for each option.
S: Select the best option: Choose the best option based on your evaluation.

Try out the DEWS decision making process with the following scenario. How can you act so that your yetzer hatov wins out? Then write your own scenario and make your decision by using the DEWS process. Did using the DEWS process help you make a good decision?

Jake's parents will be away for the weekend and his friends think this is a great time to party at his house. Jake knows his parents think he is very responsible and trustworthy. In fact, Jake's father told him that because he is so responsible, they are going to buy him his own car next summer. Jake isn't sure just how wild his friends will be at the party, but knows they will want to have alcohol at it. Jake's friends think he doesn't have any guts because he is reluctant to have the party at his house and keep telling him how great it will be and how they'll clean everything up.

Define the dilemma: _____

Explore the options:
1.
2.
3.

Weigh the consequences:

	Pros	Cons
Option 1:		
Option 2:		
Option 3:		

Select the best option: _____

Responsibility: Actions Have Consequences

Every person is responsible for his or her actions, and for the consequences of those actions. Think back to our conversation about being forgiven for our sins—we must fix any harm we have caused with our friends before God will forgive—because we are responsible for those actions we took that caused the harm.

Responsibility means _____.

In the aftermath of a bad decision, people will often use the excuse "Oh, I didn't think that would happen." Unfortunately, not having thought through to the consequences of an action is not an excuse. Our choices may have short-term and long-term consequences—and while the short-term consequence may feel good at the moment, the longer-term consequence may have a terrible impact.

Scenario 3

Think for example about Sam and Sami, two friends who are partying together and decide on the spur of the moment to 'hook up'. Sami has just broken up with her boyfriend Todd because he was pressuring her to have sex and she didn't want to. Now at the party, she has been drinking and feeling lonely and sorry for herself. When Sam, a boy she knows since kindergarten sees her, he suggests that if they hook up she won't feel so badly. Sami feels safe with Sam and is disgusted with herself for being such a "prude" with Todd. She decides to go for it and they hook up. It feels good and Sami can barely remember why she had said no to Todd. The next day however after her hangover wears off, Sami is back to reality and has to look at herself in the mirror. Instead of feeling good, she feels degraded and upset with herself and worried.

What do you think she might be worried about?
What can she do about that now?
How might this all have been avoided?

What are possible short- and long-term consequences for Sami? Think about STDs, pregnancy, how she views herself and her reputation. What about Sam? Are there short- and long-term consequences for him? Are the consequences different for guys than for girls? Why and how might they be different?

It is human nature to act impulsively, to speak or act before we think. Let's look at a text where a person acted without thinking, benefited from the short-term consequences and paid a big price for the long-term consequences.

Let's examine the narrative of Adam and Eve and the fruit—Bereishit 3:1-13. This is a well known text but let's take a look at it through the lens of relationships, peer pressure, and short and long term consequences.

א וְהַנָּחָשׁ, הָיָה עָרוּם, מִכֹּל חַיַּת הַשָּׂדֶה, אֲשֶׁר עָשָׂה יְהוָה אֱלֹהִים; וַיֹּאמֶר, אֶל-הָאִשָּׁה, אַף כִּי-אָמַר אֱלֹהִים, לֹא תֹאכְלוּ מִכֹּל עֵץ הַגָּן.

1 Now the serpent was more subtle than any beast of the field which the Lord God had made. And he said unto the woman: 'God said: You shall not eat of any tree of the garden?'

ב וַתֹּאמֶר הָאִשָּׁה, אֶל-הַנָּחָשׁ: מִפְּרִי עֵץ-הַגָּן, נֹאכֵל. ג וּמִפְּרִי הָעֵץ, אֲשֶׁר בְּתוֹךְ-הַגָּן--אָמַר אֱלֹהִים לֹא תֹאכְלוּ מִמֶּנּוּ, וְלֹא תִגְּעוּ בּוֹ: פֶּן-תְּמֻתוּן.

2 And the woman said unto the serpent: 'Of the fruit of the trees of the garden we may eat; 3 but of the fruit of the tree which is in the midst of the garden, God said: You shall not eat of it, neither shall you touch it, lest you die.'

ד וַיֹּאמֶר הַנָּחָשׁ, אֶל-הָאִשָּׁה: לֹא-מוֹת, תְּמֻתוּן. ה כִּי, יֹדֵעַ אֱלֹהִים, כִּי בְּיוֹם אֲכָלְכֶם מִמֶּנּוּ, וְנִפְקְחוּ עֵינֵיכֶם; וִהְיִיתֶם, כֵּאלֹהִים, יֹדְעֵי, טוֹב וָרָע.

4 And the serpent said unto the woman: 'You shall not surely die; 5 for God doesn't know that in the day you eat thereof, then your eyes shall be opened, and you shall be as God, knowing good and evil.'

ו וַתֵּרֶא הָאִשָּׁה כִּי טוֹב הָעֵץ לְמַאֲכָל וְכִי תַאֲוָה-הוּא לָעֵינַיִם, וְנֶחְמָד הָעֵץ לְהַשְׂכִּיל, וַתִּקַּח מִפִּרְיוֹ, וַתֹּאכַל; וַתִּתֵּן גַּם-לְאִישָׁהּ עִמָּהּ, וַיֹּאכַל.

6 And when the woman saw that the tree was good for food, and that it was a delight to the eyes, and that the tree was to be desired to make one wise, she took of the fruit thereof, and did eat; and she gave also unto her husband with her, and he did eat.

ז וַתִּפָּקַחְנָה, עֵינֵי שְׁנֵיהֶם, וַיֵּדְעוּ, כִּי עֵירֻמִּם הֵם; וַיִּתְפְּרוּ עֲלֵה תְאֵנָה, וַיַּעֲשׂוּ לָהֶם חֲגֹרֹת.

7 And the eyes of both of them were opened, and they knew that they were naked; and they sewed fig-leaves together, and made themselves girdles.

ח וַיִּשְׁמְעוּ אֶת-קוֹל יְהוָה אֱלֹהִים, מִתְהַלֵּךְ בַּגָּן--לְרוּחַ הַיּוֹם; וַיִּתְחַבֵּא הָאָדָם וְאִשְׁתּוֹ, מִפְּנֵי יְהוָה אֱלֹהִים, בְּתוֹךְ, עֵץ הַגָּן.

8 And they heard the voice of the Lord God walking in the garden toward the cool of the day; and the man and his wife hid themselves from the presence of the Lord God amongst the trees of the garden.

ט וַיִּקְרָא יְהוָה אֱלֹהִים, אֶל-הָאָדָם; וַיֹּאמֶר לוֹ, אַיֶּכָּה. י וַיֹּאמֶר, אֶת-קֹלְךָ שָׁמַעְתִּי בַּגָּן; וָאִירָא כִּי-עֵירֹם אָנֹכִי, וָאֵחָבֵא.

9 And the Lord God called to the man, and said to him: 'Where are you?' 10 And he said: 'I heard Your voice in the garden, and I was afraid, because I was naked; and I hid myself.'

יא **וַיֹּאמֶר--מִי הִגִּיד לְךָ, כִּי עֵירֹם אָתָּה;** הֲמִן-הָעֵץ, אֲשֶׁר צִוִּיתִיךָ לְבִלְתִּי אֲכָל-מִמֶּנּוּ-- אָכָלְתָּ.

יב **וַיֹּאמֶר, הָאָדָם: הָאִשָּׁה אֲשֶׁר נָתַתָּה** עִמָּדִי, הִוא נָתְנָה-לִּי מִן-הָעֵץ וָאֹכֵל.

יג **וַיֹּאמֶר יְהוָה אֱלֹהִים לָאִשָּׁה, מַה-זֹּאת** עָשִׂית; וַתֹּאמֶר, הָאִשָּׁה, הַנָּחָשׁ הִשִּׁיאַנִי, וָאֹכֵל.

11 And God said: 'Who told you that you were naked? Have you eaten of the tree, whereof I commanded you that you should not eat?'

12 And the man said: 'The woman whom you gave to be with me, she gave me of the tree, and I did eat.'

13 And the Lord God said to the woman: 'What is this you have done?' And the woman said: 'The serpent beguiled me, and I did eat.'

The tree in the middle of the garden is something that is forbidden—think of what that might be in the context of a relationship—for example, maybe it is forbidden and/or inappropriate sex. The snake is someone posing as a 'friend'—but who is actually trying to make you do something that is the wrong thing to do. Eve chooses to do what the snake is urging her to do, disregarding what she knows God told her because it would taste good, it looked good, and it would enlighten her— (l'haskeel) even though she knew it was the wrong thing to do. She did what was forbidden and she gave some to her partner Adam who was with her (and presumably therefore knew what was going on) and he ate also.

What was the short-term consequence of Eve and Adam's actions? Did they enjoy the fruit? We don't know, the text doesn't say. But it does say that it changed the way they looked at the world and it changed the way they were able **to be** in the world. They also immediately knew that what they did was wrong, as they hid from God when God called.

Let's look at Adam's response to God when asked if he ate from the tree. Rather than starting out his answer to God with a yes or a no, he immediately blames Eve for his actions. And Eve blames the snake for her actions. No one is taking responsibility for what he or she did. But let's look at this further. Perhaps Adam trusted Eve and didn't question her, because after all, God gave him Eve as his helpmate, his partner. And perhaps Eve trusted the snake because after all, he was a snake and was convincing and wily while posing as a friend. And while it would be wonderful to be able to think that our friends, our partners, always have our best interests at heart, we each need to listen to our 'gut' when we are making important choices about how we act and what we do.

What does this story teach us about consequences and responsibility? Do you think the Torah begins with this type of story to teach us the power of choice and the effects of our actions for a reason?

What were the long-term consequences for each of the players? They were never able to return to the state of being they had enjoyed before these actions. What they did has changed them forever.

It is important to pay attention to the choices you make, and to try and think things through using the DEWS process. Of course you won't have time to map out every decision you make, but if you remember those steps and try to incorporate them into your everyday life, it can help to ensure that you will make good decisions.

Another idea is to talk a decision through with someone else, like a friend or a trusted adult. Sometimes talking through a dilemma can help clarify the decision making process.

Challenges to Good Decision Making

Decision making, when laid out clearly in a chart, seems like it can be pretty easy. But it's not always so simple, and you won't always have time to think things through so fully. You're posed with dilemmas every day, and sometimes have to make split-second decisions about them. In addition, there may be other factors that influence your decision making.

What other factors can influence decision making?

Your choice, your life: you have an immense amount of authority and responsibility given to you through the power of free will. You have the ability to control your negative influences by exercising your right and your ability to consider your options, be influenced by the right people and make an informed, aware decision. Your decision making ability comes from a number of sources but as a teen, your most dominant and significant source of your decisions come from your friends. Peer pressure is often a major factor in how we make decisions. Being thoughtful and confident about important decisions before making them is important and there are some helpful tools for that purpose. Thinking through the short- and long-term consequences is really important before making any decision. It is your right and your ability to choose what is best for you choose wisely!

So, do I have a choice? What should young Jews choose?

Even though you can (and should) be guided by Jewish values and morals in making the important decisions in life, the reality is that you are influenced by much more than that. No one but you will decide what you do, but as a Jew, consider the concept of *Kedusha* in making decisions about your body and soul. There is enough pressure from the outside to not know yourself on the inside. Make decisions that are healthy for you as an individual, that reflect your feelings and your beliefs.

Conclusion

Throughout this book, we have examined the different components to building healthy relationships through a Jewish perspective. We've discussed the ways the Jewish people are interconnected, the importance of establishing and maintaining our relationships with others, the importance of equality and partnership in relationships, the supportive power of friendship, how we are all individuals, the sanctity of intimacy, and how to be a friend to someone in an unhealthy relationship. Throughout our entire discussion, we've focused on the concept of choices and helped you recognize your ability and right to choose how you respond to situations.

Healthy relationships, whether they are friendships or dating relationships, are critical to our health and safety and social and emotional well-being, and unhealthy relationships are harmful. It is important to surround ourselves with supportive friends, and to be a supportive friend to others.

Healthy relationships are characterized by trust, good communication, and equality and partnership. Whether it be bein adam l'makom (God), bein adam l'atzmo (self) or bein adam l'chavero (between others), healthy relationships are supportive and make us feel loved and respected.

Activity: My Steps From Here

On the lines attached to each footprint, write out the "steps" you'll take to reflect how what you've learned will affect your behavior. Do you think differently at all in terms of your relationship with God, yourself and others? How will your behavior reflect that? What steps will you take?

Final Steps: I've learned...

On the this page, write, draw, or glue! Use magazine cut-outs words or an image to show your definition of a healthy relationship. Or, write an analogy that compares healthy relationships to something real.

For example, A healthy relationship is like a being a co-captain on a ship. Some days, the waters are choppy, and you have to work together to beat the wind, sail through the storms, dance on the deck and appreciate the journey as beautiful!

A healthy relationship is:

Bibliography

Borowitz, Eugene and Frances Weinman Schwartz, *Jewish Moral Virtues*. Philadelphia, PA: Jewish Publication Society, 1999.

Dorff, Rabbi Elliot N., *This is My Beloved, This is My Friend: A Rabbinic Letter on Intimate Relations*. New York, NY: The Rabbinical Assembly, 1996.

Gardsbane, Diane, ed., *Embracing Justice: A Resource Guide for Rabbis on Domestic Abuse*. Washington, DC: Jewish Women International, 2002.

Greenfeld, Jay M., *My Choice, My Life: Realizing Your Abililty to Create Balance in Life*. Denver, CO: Outskirtspress, 2009.

Isaacs, Rabbi Ronald, *Derech Eretz: The Path to an Ethical Life*. New York, NY: United Synagogue of Conservative Judaism, 1995.

Kieffer, Rabbi Sam, *The Jewish Lifecycle*. New York, NY: United Synagogue of Conservative Judaism, revised edition, 2003.

Kivel, Paul, *Men's Work: How to Stop the Violence That Tears Our Lives Apart*. Center City, MN: Hazelden Publishing, 1992, rev. 1998.

Novick, Bernard, *In God's Image: Making Jewish Decisions about the Body*. New York, NY: United Synagogue of Conservative Judaism, 1994.

Parker-Pope, Tara, *Bullying, Suicide Risk for Victims and Tormentors*, **citing the International Journal of Adolescent Medicine and Health.**

Sex and Tech: Results from a Survey of Teens and Young Adults.
The National Campaign to Prevent Teen and Unplanned Pregnancy and CosmoGirl.com, 2008.

Tabachnick, Joan, *Engaging Bystanders in Sexual Violence Prevention*. Enola, PA: National Sexual Violence Resource Center, 2009.

Tech Abuse in Teen Relationships: A Study. Liz Claiborne Inc., 2007

Make Your Child Bully Proof. The Heroes and Dreams Foundation, 2009

NOtes

NOtes

Notes